PULLING DOWN
STRONGHOLDS

PULLING DOWN
STRONGHOLDS

DR. HECTOR P. TORRES

Pulling Down Strongholds
Copyright © 1999
by Hector Torres
ISBN 0-9667481-6-6

Published by
Wagner Institute for Practical Ministry
P.O. Box 62958
Colorado Springs, CO 80962-2958

Previously published in Spanish *"Derribemos Fortalezas"* ©1993
Editorial Betania (Revised)
P.O. Box 141000
Nashville, TN 37214-1000

Rights for publishing this book in other languages are contracted by Gospel Literature International (GLINT). GLINT also provides technical help for the adaptation, translation, and publishing of Bible study resources and books in scores of languages worldwide. For further information, contact GLINT, P.O. Box 4060, Ontario, CA 91761-1003, USA, Email: glintint@aol.com, or the publisher.

ACKNOWLEDGEMENTS

This book was made possible through the prayers, support, and love in Christ of Cindy Jacobs, Dr. C. Peter Wagner, and my Pastor, Gary Kinnaman. They have been instruments used by God to impact my life and my spiritual understanding.

On June 13, 1990, I received an invitation from Dr. C. Peter Wagner to participate in The Spiritual Warfare Network which had its origin in the prayer movement which took place July, 1989 at Lausanne II in Manila, Philippines.

Much of the information contained in this book was compiled by gathering shared information through the network that held conferences on spiritual warfare in Argentina, Colombia, Ecuador, Mexico, the Philippines, Uruguay, and the United States. I would also like to thank the ministry of intercession at my home church, Word of Grace, for their many prayers on my behalf. In particular, I thank Nancy Austin for the extensive and excellent work she has done in editing this manuscript.

DEDICATION

I dedicate this book to my wife, Myriam, whose prayers and love have upheld me for more than twenty-nine years, and to my brother Gabriel who led me to the Savior and has been a source of support for my ministry throughout the years.

TABLE OF CONTENTS

This book will be of great use to the American Church in the coming years.

Perhaps not everyone will agree with every position the author takes in this book, yet we will all agree on the reality of the battles that take place in the spiritual realm. If we do not develop the spiritual discernment needed to face the powers of darkness, we will not be able to reach key people in key cities and territories.

In the past, the Church has been perceived in several forms; we have distinguished it to be a body, a people, or a family. Presently, we see the church emerging as an army, unrestrained, invincible, warring, and winning in Jesus' name! Should the Lord tarry, the Church in America will be a different Church by the year 2000. Actually, we are raising a new generation of Christians. They're in love with Jesus, they bear Calvary's indelible imprints, and they know and use the authority of the name of Jesus.

With great joy, I introduce this book written by my good friend and colleague, Dr. Hector Torres, a contemporary spiritual preacher and vibrant leader.

Dr. Alberto H. Mottesi
Evangelist

FOREWORD

———◆———

What is the Holy Spirit saying to the church today? Surely He is saying many things, for we live at a crucial time for the advancement of the kingdom of God. Among all His messages, we hear one recurring theme, "Church, prepare yourself for battle."

This battle is spiritual. Because we live in a great decade for the harvest of souls and that harvest increases year after year, Satan is coming against the advance of the gospel ferociously. All the faithful followers of the Lord must arise to battle.

This battle is neither child's play nor a past-time for the curious. It is serious business. Although the outcome is certain — Jesus Christ defeated Satan and the forces of darkness on Calvary's cross — the struggle has not ended and will not end until Jesus comes again. Therefore, He commands us to face the enemy and to know that we may experience victories and losses while engaging in battle. Some are afraid to fight.

They prefer the comfort of their church buildings instead of the conflicts of their world. My good friend, Hector Torres, is not among them. With the courage of David confronting the mighty Goliath, he has come to the forefront of the battle. *Pulling Down Strongholds* is an inspiring book in which the author shares not only what he has learned theoretically, but what he has acquired through experience.

This book could be an instrument in God's hands to accelerate the evangelization of your community, your state, and all of your nation. Hector Torres's teachings on spiritual warfare are timely. This is the time for the greatest harvest of souls known to Christian history. Now is the time for spiritual warfare. You will not be able to find a better book to prepare you for the battle than *Pulling Down Strongholds*.

Dr. C. Peter Wagner
President, Global Harvest Ministries
Colorado Springs, Colorado

INTRODUCTION

"And I saw the beast, the kings of the earth, and their armies, gathered together to make war against Him who sat on the horse and against His army."
(Revelation 19:19)

There is no doubt that the day of the Lord is quickly approaching. Satan, the prince of the power of the air, and his armies have wreaked havoc on the earth and amongst mankind. The inhabitants of the earth are uniting against the Lord and His church! Yet the Commander in Chief of God's army is calling His Church together, enabling it to be equipped, strengthened, and fortified, so that it may rise up ready for battle!

The prophet Joel gives an analogy of today's army as he writes that there will be a powerful and numerous people. The heathen nations will tremble before this great and mighty army. They will turn white with fear because of this undaunted army's power to destroy anything that gets in its way. It shall be an army that does not break ranks and is clear in its purpose. The Lord will execute the command to attack. His army is great and powerful!

Isaiah calls a sleeping people to awaken and to arise so

that the glory of the Lord may be revealed throughout the land! Paul states that the creation anxiously waits for the manifestation of the sons of God. God's prophetic message for today's church is to unite in preparation for the work of ministry. Once trained and prepared for battle, the Church will declare war against the powers of darkness and destroy the works of evil.

"Proclaim this among the nations; **Prepare for war!** Wake-up the mighty men, *let all the men of war draw near, let them come up.* Beat your plowshares into swords, and your pruning hooks into spears; let the weak say, 'I am strong.' Assemble and come, all you nations, and gather together all around. Cause Your mighty ones to go down there, O Lord. Let the nations be wakened, and come up to the valley of Jehoshaphat; for there I will sit to judge all the surrounding nations. Put in the sickle, for the harvest is ripe. Come, go down; for the winepress is full, the vats overflow- for their wickedness is great. Multitudes, multitudes in the valley of decision! *For the day of the Lord is near in the valley of decision*" (Joel 3:9-14 bold and italics added.)

The purpose of this book is to prepare the Church for this call of God. God's people have been victimized due to ignorance. It is time to WAKE UP, to arise as an army ready to do battle against the powers of evil. "Who will rise up for me against the evildoers? Who will stand up for me against the workers of iniquity?" (Psalm 94:16)

The Church of Jesus Christ has been called to discern the times, to proclaim and disseminate the revelation that it has received from God to equip the saints. As guardians of God's truth, we need to declare, write, and record the things we see, so that the people will read about them (see Habakkuk 2:2). George Otis, Jr. states in his book, *The Last of the Giants,* that "the Church of Jesus Christ is God's main vehicle for revelation on the earth today. This statement contains three elements that are crucial for the church to understand:

1. The times in which we live.
2. The battlefields in which we fight.
3. God's methods for evangelism and spiritual warfare." [1]

This book is divided into three parts:
1. Spiritual warfare against the family
2. Spiritual warfare against the church
3. Spiritual warfare against nations

My desire is to identify the three battlefields, as well as the weapons God has given us to Pull Down the Strongholds built by hell's armies throughout the centuries. Using the techniques of spiritual mapping and intercession, we will endeavor to identify spiritual strongholds that have ruled over territories and have established borders around the world.

God is raising up a group of men and women who, like the sons of Issachar, are called to discern the times, take advantage of opportunities, and expound on the steps the Church must take in this spiritual conflict.

> "...of the sons of Issachar who had understanding of the times, to know what Israel ought to do... and all their brethren were at their command"
> (1 Chronicles 12:32).

Notes
[1] George Otis Jr., *The Last of the Giants.* Grand Rapids MI: Chosen Books, 1991, pp. 34-35.

PART ONE

SPIRITUAL WARFARE

"And the dragon was enraged with the woman, and he went to make war with the rest of her offspring, who keep the commandments of God and have the testimony of Jesus Christ."

(Revelation 12:17)

CHAPTER ONE

THE SPIRITUAL BATTLE

Throughout the Christian world there is a wave of interest in the supernatural, along with a growing concern regarding the topic of spiritual warfare. Numerous theological seminaries along with both independent and denominational churches have begun studies on the subjects of power evangelism, healing, and deliverance. As a result, great interest has been stirred in three main areas:

1. Intercession to break yokes and bring healing and deliverance.
2. Intercession for Christian leadership and the Church.
3. The direct relationship between intercessory prayer and church growth (evangelism).

I am fully convinced that God's call to the Church at this time is to equip the saints for spiritual warfare so they may reach the whole world before the return of Christ through "power evangelism."

There are apparently three different levels of spiritual warfare.[1]

PERSONAL LEVEL SPIRITUAL WARFARE
(PERSONAL STRONGHOLDS)

This is the most common level and the one in which the Church has primarily operated in the past. It represents Satan's conflict against individual humans and the family structure, which is the base and foundation of mankind. On this level, we are battling personal strongholds. These strongholds are things that Satan uses to influence someone's personal life, such as: sinful thoughts, feelings, attitudes, and personal styles of discipline.[2]

> "And when He had called His twelve disciples to Him, He gave them power over unclean spirits, to cast them out, and to heal all kinds of sickness and all kinds of disease." (Matthew 10:1)

> "For unclean spirits, crying with a loud voice, came out of many who were possessed; and many who were paralyzed and lame were healed." (Acts 8:7)

Because of the high involvement in spiritism, witchcraft, and the occult, it is inconceivable that evangelism in many areas of the world could be effective without the ministry of deliverance accompanied by the preaching of God's Word. The truth is that "power evangelism" cannot be successful without some measure of deliverance. Because of this, a number of groups and individuals have surfaced with deliverance ministries, especially among Charismatics and Pentecostals.

IDEOLOGICAL LEVEL SPIRITUAL WARFARE
(IDEOLOGICAL STRONGHOLDS)

At this level, the enemy uses ideological or philosophical strongholds and is known to operate by means of false religions and doctrines of witchcraft, Satanism, voodoo, spiritism, necromancy, sorcery, magic, astrology, and mediums, etc. These ideologies are philosophies used by Satan to influence culture and society. Confrontations at this level are unlike those at personal level warfare that come against unclean spirits of lust, gluttony, drunkenness, etc., which are personal strongholds.

The Bible gives us at least one example of a spirit at this level that caused great political commotion, incited a multitude to violence, and led local authorities to rise against God's Church.

"Now it happened, as we went to prayer, that a certain slave girl possessed with a spirit of divination met us, who brought her masters much profit by fortune-telling. This girl followed Paul and us, and cried out saying, 'These men are the servants of the Most High God, who proclaim to us the way of salvation.' And this she did for many days, but Paul, greatly annoyed, turned and said to the spirit, 'I command you in the name of Jesus to come out of her.' And he came out that very hour. But when her masters saw that their hope of profit was gone, they seized Paul and Silas and dragged them into the marketplace to the authorities. And they brought them to the magistrates, and said, 'These men, being Jews, exceedingly trouble our city; and they teach customs which are not lawful for us, being Romans, to receive or observe.' Then the multitude rose up together against them; and the magistrates tore off their clothes and commanded them to be beaten with rods. And when they had laid many stripes on them they threw them into prison, commanding the jailer to keep them securely. Having received such a charge, he put them into the inner prison and fastened their feet in the stocks" (Acts 16:16-24)

This level of spiritual warfare exists and is loosed to destroy the Church, pastors, and ministries and hinder the work of evangelism. Furthermore, these forces blind people to the truth of the gospel message, to demonic activity, and to the reality of spiritual darkness.

In his book *Warfare Prayer,* Dr. C. Peter Wagner says that in Germany there are more witches registered in government registries than there are Christian ministers. Also, a missionary in France says the majority of the French consult witch doctors rather than professional doctors. It is of utmost importance to know that Satanism is the fastest growing religion in most parts of the world. [4]

A few years ago, more than eighteen bodies were found in Matamoros, Mexico. All the bodies were victims of satanic rituals performed by drug lords seeking Satan's protection from local drug enforcement agencies.

The immigration of Cubans and Haitians to Miami, Florida, brought with them an invasion of Santeria priests and voodoo adherents. *Santeria* is a form of spiritism. Daily, children are victimized by the rituals of human sacrifice - like those performed to Baal - and the bodies of dead cats, dogs, and headless birds are found along Miami's water canals. Santeria has gained such power that the State of Florida and city governments have officially met with Santeros (Santeria priests) to help calm tensions between police and minorities.

"Nancy Reagan, former President Ronald Reagan's wife, drew much attention to herself when she consulted with an astrologer concerning guidance on making a worldwide political decision. Also, Michael Dukakis, the ex-Presidential candidate from the state of Massachusetts, named a woman as the official 'witch' of his state."[5]

IT IS OF UTMOST IMPORTANCE TO KNOW THAT
SATANISM IS THE FASTEST GROWING
RELIGION IN MOST PARTS OF THE WORLD

Dr. Wagner elaborates on the decline of Argentina saying that Argentina had experienced the least amount of spiritual revival in the Latin-American nations. However, in the 1982 Falkland War, the Argentineans, known internationally for their pride, suffered a terrible defeat to England before the whole world. With their pride crushed, Argentineans saw that their military and religion had failed them, so they began to seek something new. Presently, Argentina is known as one of the three Latin-American nations with the greatest church growth. What happened in Argentina? How did Argentina go from the least experienced in spiritual revival to being one of the fastest church-growing nations in Latin-America?

In the 60's and 70's, Argentina, a prosperous and economically strong nation, was considered by many to be the jewel of South America. However, it began to weaken when Argentina's President, Juan Domingo Peron, began to associate with a powerful occultist named Jose Lopez Rega, popularly known as 'El Brujo' (the Warlock). During this time, Peron appointed El Brujo to serve as his minister of social benefits. When Peron died in 1974, El Brujo became the private counselor of Peron's wife, Isabel. During her two years of

Presidency, Isabel allowed El Brujo to build public monuments to witchcraft, bringing a curse on Argentina; they've all since been destroyed. When the military overthrew Isabel in 1976, El Brujo publicly cursed the nation of Argentina. [6]

In spite of the Brazilian spiritism known as 'Macumba' invading areas of Argentina and Uruguay, the local Uruguayan church grew more than 25 percent in November 1991 during evangelistic crusades held in Fray Bentos. Because of these crusades, many miracles and deliverances were observed. During this time, the 'Macumberos,' adherents of Macumba, ransacked a local Baptist church for three consecutive days, destroying doors, windows, and leaving walls and furniture contaminated with feces. Nevertheless, the city of Fray Bentos experienced spiritual revival and unity among the clergy.

The Argentine magazine *Somos* recently reported that President Carlos Menen regularly consults his personal witch, Ilda Evelia, who has been retained for 28 years. The magazine further quotes a high ranking government official with the following, "The truth is that the majority of us frequently consult witches."[7]

TERRITORIAL LEVEL SPIRITUAL WARFARE; SPIRITUAL MAPPING (TERRITORIAL STRONGHOLDS)

In this level, the enemy uses territorial strongholds. These strongholds represent evil hierarchies that are strategically placed and assigned by Satan himself to influence and control nations, communities, and the family. Additionally, certain demonic forces gather together in different cities to strengthen various types of wickedness. In specific cities there will be strongholds of idolatry, generational sins, and other types of religious spirits. Opposition is very strong at this level. The concentrated force of demonic activity, called dominions and thrones, are assigned as "territorial spirits." This type of warfare is more intense than that of casting out a demon of lust or battling against the spirit of 'Santeria' or 'Macumba.'

"For by Him all things were created that are in heaven and that are in earth, visible and invisible, whether thrones or dominions or principalities or powers. All things were created through Him and for Him." (Colossians 1:16)

"And war broke out in heaven; Michael and his angels fought with the dragon; and the dragon and his angels fought." (Revelation 12:7)

"Then he said to me, "Do not fear, Daniel, for from the first day that you set your heart to understand, and to humble yourself before your God, your words were heard; and I have come because of your words. But the prince of the kingdom of Persia withstood me twenty-one days; and behold, Michael, one of the chief princes, came to help me, for I had been left alone there with the kings of Persia." (Daniel 10:12-13)

"And he said, 'O man greatly beloved, fear not! Peace be to you; be strong, yes, be strong!' So when he spoke to me I was strengthened, and said, 'Let my Lord speak, for you have strengthened me.' Then he said, 'Do you know why I have come to you? And now I must return to fight with the prince of Persia; and when I have gone forth, indeed the prince of Greece will come. But I will tell you what is noted in the scripture of truth; and there is none that upholds me against these, except Michael your prince.'" (Daniel 10:19-21)

"In which you once walked according to the course of this world, according to the prince of the power of the air, the spirit who now works in the sons of disobedience." (Ephesians 2:2)

"I know your works, and where you dwell, where Satan's throne is. And you hold fast to My name, and did not deny My faith even in the days in which Antipas was My faithful martyr, who was killed among you, where Satan dwells." (Revelation 2:13)

After his conversion, an ex-member of the Colombian 'Guerilla' told Dr. Alberto Mottesi the following incident: In Colombia, the Guerillas tried repeatedly to overthrow the town of El Bagre. However, every audacious attempt was hindered. Being very superstitious, the Guerillas went to consult a witch in an attempt to find out why their assault plans were unsuccessful. The witch told them that two small evangelical churches met on a weekly basis, faithfully praying for the town and for God's protection. The witch's last comment was, "While they continue in unity and prayer, you will not be able to accomplish your objective."

Why did Jesus come?
"...for this purpose the Son of God was manifested, that He might destroy the works of the devil."
(1 John 3:8 italics added)

"...for the Son of Man has come to seek and to save that which was lost." (Luke 19:10 italics added)

What is the purpose of spiritual warfare?
To involve the Church in the battle and intercession to:
1. Break yokes and bondage; to bring physical and emotional healing and deliverance.
2. Protect and cover the local, national, and universal Church against the attacks of the enemy.
3. Produce a harvest of lost souls through power and mass evangelism.

What are the three levels of spiritual warfare?
1. Personal Level: personal strongholds
2. Ideological Level: ideological or philosophical strongholds
3. Territorial Level: territorial strongholds

DEFINITIONS

STRONGHOLD(S) - personal
1. A predisposed mind, impregnated with hopelessness, which leads a believer in Christ to accept the fact that he/she cannot change situations or circumstances, even though these are contrary to God's will.[8]
2. My definition of a personal stronghold(s) is, "Anything that hinders you from doing or being what God says you can do or be."
3. The limitations imposed on individuals by spoken words or by the actions of others.
4. Mind-sets of people in a particular territory that are fortified places keeping out the truth and holding in lies. [9]

STRONGHOLD(S) - philosophical
False philosophical doctrines that Satan uses to keep people under deception. Their primary objective is to keep people from seeing the light of the Gospel and divide the Church.

STRONGHOLD(S) - territorial

Fortresses that Satan builds to exalt himself against the wisdom and plans of God (2 Corinthians 10:4). From the Greek word *ochuroma,* meaning a fortress, a castle, or a fortified place. [10]

SPIRIT(S)

1. A dwelling place for emotions and feelings. Mental disposition or mind set (e.g., spirit of fear, spirit of lust, spirit of faith).
2. Pneuma, the sentient element in man, by which he perceives, reflects, feels, desires (not senses).
3. Supernatural spirits; angels or demons (e.g., spirit of divination).
4. Divine Spirit; God's Holy Spirit.

Notes

[1] Dr. C. Peter Wagner, *Warfare Prayer.* Ventura CA: Regal Books, 1990, p. 16.

[2] Gary Kinnaman, *Overcoming the Dominion of Darkness.* Grand Rapids MI: Chosen Books, 1990, p. 58

[3] Wagner, p. 3.

[4] Ibid, p. 19.

[5] Ibid, p. 17.

[6] Ibid, p. 22-24.

[7] Ibid, p. 24.

[8] Edgardo Silvoso, *Plan Resistencia*, Presented to the Spiritual Warfare Network Meeting, Pasadena California November 1990.

[9] John Eckhardt, *Moving in the Apostolic.* Ventura CA: Renew Books, 1999, p.58.

[10] Ibid, p. 58.

CHAPTER TWO

THE CHURCH'S PURPOSE

The eyes of your understanding being enlightened; that you may know what is the hope of His calling, what are the riches of the glory of His inheritance in the saints, and what is the exceeding greatness of His power toward us who believe, according to the working of His mighty power which He worked in Christ when He raised Him from the dead and seated Him at His right hand in the heavenly places, far above all principality and power and might and dominion and every name that is named, not only in this age, but also in that which is to come and He put all things under His feet, and gave Him to be head over all things to the Church which is His body, the fullness of Him who fills all in all. (Ephesians 1:18-23)

The Church has been called to recognize and declare that all the power of the enemy is under the feet of Jesus. Yet to see this fulfilled, we must know the adversary and we must prepare a strategy to block his attack. We must also know that Satan's purpose is to hinder God's people from working in the authority, power, and anointing given to them by God through His Holy Spirit.

God calls us to be agents of change in the world, not people changed by the world. When we take our eyes off of the Lord and put them on ourselves, it is easy to lose focus and the vision God has given us.

AS HUMANS, WE ALL SEEK FOUR THINGS

Comfort: We obtain this by material possessions, prestige and, entertainment.

Security: We try to do away with insecurity and fear through the accumulation of possessions and surround ourselves with all types of resources to protect us in difficult times.

Self-acceptance: We desire to be accepted and loved by others only with the purpose of self-gratification, even in ministry.

Self-love: We do all in our power to have our own way, putting ourselves before others. We will sacrifice only if in doing so we are benefited, never considering how our actions affect others.

WHAT WE SHOULD DO AS CHRISTIANS

Be servants: We should serve others so that their lives will be meaningful. Rejoice in knowing that we are helping others and we will receive from the Lord our just reward. The servant of God serves others.

Be disciples: We need to have faith and trust in His promises that say He will provide and that God is aware of our needs and will answer accordingly. Also, learning to walk in the promises of God is being a disciple.

Be ministers: Love others in spite of their faults even as God loved us while we were lost in sin. Every work of ministry is based on the compassion that we feel for human suffering.

Be priests: Communion with God and offering sacrifices of praise are all part of being a priest.

As Christians, when we focus on these four areas, we are able to achieve the objectives set forth by Jesus Christ through the Holy Spirit to fulfill the Great Commission.

> "Now all things are of God, who has reconciled us to Himself through Jesus Christ, and has given us the ministry of reconciliation, that is that God was in Christ reconciling the world to Himself, not imputing their trespasses to them, and has committed to us the word of reconciliation. Now then, we are ambassadors for Christ, as though God were pleading through us; we implore you on Christ's behalf, be reconciled to God."   (2 Corinthians 5:18-20)

GOD'S REQUIREMENTS FOR HIS CHURCH

1. **Win souls for Jesus** (impact).
    "And He said to them, 'Go into all the world and preach the gospel to every creature'" (Mark 16:15).
2. **Make disciples** (excellence).
    "And Jesus came and spoke to them, saying, 'All authority has been given to Me in heaven and on earth. Go therefore make disciples of all the nations, baptizing them in the name of the Father and of the Son and of the Holy Spirit, teaching them to observe all things that I have commanded you; and lo, I am with you always, even to the end of the age.' Amen" (Matthew 28:18-20).

What is the definition of a disciple? A disciple is a worshiper obedient to the Word of God, a servant of God and man, a teachable person, and one who embraces a life of repentance.

What We Should Do As Disciples

Equip the saints for battle (mobilization).
"And He Himself gave some to be apostles, some prophets, some evangelists, and some pastors and teachers, for the equipping of the saints, for the work of ministry, for the edifying of the body of Christ, till we all come to the unity of the faith and of the knowledge of the Son of God, to a perfect man, to the measure of the stature of the fullness of Christ; that we should no longer be children, tossed to and fro and carried about with every wind of doctrine, by the   trickery of men, in the cunning craftiness of deceitful plotting, but, speaking the truth in love, may grow up in all things into Him who is the head- Christ- from whom the whole body, joined and knit together by what every joint supplies, according to the effective working by which every part does it's share, causes growth of the body for the edifying of itself in love" (Ephesians 4:11-16).

Bring the Church into a *true* unity of the Spirit. We must make every effort to establish a Christian community, to destroy barriers of division among the Church, to remove all denominational and ministerial barriers, and to battle together in unity to achieve God's purpose for the Church, the fulfillment of the *Great Commission.*

Renew Christian Holiness. We are called to be like open letters and as such our lives must be role models as imitators of Christ.
"You are our epistle written in our hearts, known and read by all men; clearly you are an epistle of Christ, ministered by us, written not with ink but by the Spirit of the living

God, not on tablets of stone but on tablets of flesh, that is, of the heart" (2 Corinthians 3:2-3).

Renew the Church's image. Many have turned their backs on the Church due to its lack of relevancy to the problems and sufferings of today's world. Primarily, this occurs within religious traditions and with minds prejudiced towards the gospel. If we are to be successful, we must remove all "religious" spirits from our congregations.

Defend Christian morals. If we do not fight against the attacks of the enemy, we will be victims of our indifference to the things of God.

The key lies in examining our priorities in ministry, in our lives, and in committing ourselves to obeying God. We need to make a covenant with God to work together with fellow believers, achieve *His* purposes, and serve Him with all our being, for His glory and not ours.

Finally, a son is one who knows his kinship, but a disciple is one who lives what he has learned; he is not only a hearer, but also a doer.

God is seeking to use *credible ministries,* not incredible ministries. Our credibility should be seen and known by the world. Our attitude and conduct are the barometer of our relationship and consecration to God.

CHAPTER THREE

OFFENSIVE WARFARE

Then Jesus, being filled with the Holy Spirit, returned from the Jordan and was led by the Spirit into the wilderness. (Luke 4:1)

Jesus' public ministry began on the strategic level of spiritual warfare. He left the example for the church and delegated the responsibility of conducting the battle he had waged.

Jesus came to earth so that He might destroy the works of the evil one. Because Jesus' attack against the enemy was on the highest level of spiritual warfare, He demonstrated that it was time for the Kingdom of God to come (1 John 3:8).

According to W. E. Vine's *Expository Dictionary of New Testament Words*, one definition of the word "desert" (*aramies*) is, *"a place of danger, of death...and of diabolical powers."* [1] In this setting, an intense battle took place in which Satan offered Jesus *"all the kingdoms of the world and their glory,"* but Jesus, being filled with the Holy Spirit, rebuked Satan. Because Satan could not oppose the power of the Holy Spirit in Jesus, he had to depart and begin to devise a different strategy that ultimately led to the death of Christ at Calvary.

Jesus disarmed the enemy's principalities and powers through His resurrection. "Having disarmed principalities and powers, He made a public spectacle of them, triumphing over them in it" (Colossians 2.15).

Jesus then gave His Church authority over the power of the enemy.

"Then the seventy returned with joy, saying, "Lord, even the demons are subject to us in Your name. And He said to them, 'I saw Satan fall like lightning from heaven. Behold, I give you the authority to trample on serpents and scorpions, and over all the power of the enemy, and nothing shall by any means hurt you. Nevertheless, do not rejoice in this, that the spirits are subject to you, but rather rejoice because your names are written in heaven.'" (Luke 10: 17-20)

Jesus sent His Holy Spirit so that we may finish the work that He began."Most assuredly, I say to you, he who believes in Me, the works that I do he will do also; and greater works than these he will do, because I go to My Father" (John 14: 12).

"As You sent Me into the world, I also have sent them into the world. And for their sakes I sanctify Myself, that they also may be sanctified by the Truth." (John 17: 18-19)

"Then comes the end, when He delivers the kingdom to God the Father when He puts an end to all rule and all authority and power. For He must reign till He has put all enemies under His feet." (1 Corinthians 15: 24-25)

However, even after the Cross, the Bible calls Satan the god of this world. "Whose minds the god of this age has blinded, who do not believe, lest the light of the gospel of the glory of Christ, who is the image of God, should shine on them" (2 Corinthians 4:4).

He is also called the prince of the power of the air; ".... in which you once walked according to the course of this world, according to the prince of the power of the air, the spirit who now works in the sons of disobedience" (Ephesians 2:2).

The Bible goes on to say that "...the whole world still lies under the sway of the wicked one." (1 John 5:19) Many attempt to enter into spiritual warfare without being adequately prepared, and as a result they fall victim to their ignorance. "My people are destroyed for the lack of knowledge" (Hosea 4.6a).

BECAUSE JESUS' ATTACK AGAINST THE ENEMY
WAS ON THE HIGHEST LEVEL OF SPIRITUAL WARFARE,
HE DEMONSTRATED THAT IT WAS TIME FOR THE
KINGDOM OF GOD TO COME

Dr. C. Peter Wagner states, "Satan's primary goal is to prevent God from being glorified." Part of Satan's objective has been accomplished when God is not glorified in an individual's life, the church, or in the cities and nations. When the lost die without God, the evil one has obtained an eternal victory." [2]

Another ploy of Satan is to attempt to make humans miserable throughout their lifetime. Scripture states that the enemy comes "to steal, kill and destroy." Just hearing about wars, crime, poverty, racism, and oppression confirms that Satan has obtained a *temporal* victory here on earth. However, the Lord has given us authority over Satan. "See, I have this day set you over the nations and over the kingdoms, to root out and to pull down, to destroy and to throw down, to build and to plant" (Jeremiah 1:I0).

In Matthew 12:29 and Mark 3:27 it says that no one can "enter a strong man's house… unless he first binds the strong man," then he can plunder his house. Also, Jesus said that from the days of John the Baptist to now, the Kingdom of God suffers violence, and the violent take it by force. The promise for God's army is in Romans 8. "Yet in all these things we are more than conquerors through Him who loved us" (Romans 8:37).

Jeremiah the prophet was given authority over nations and kingdoms as an intercessor in the spiritual realm. "Kingdoms" are those that reign in the spiritual realm over an invisible arena. "Nations" refers to the secular leadership over visible areas."[3]

Notes

[1] W. E. Vine's *Expository Dictionary of NewTestament Words,* Fleming H. Revell Company.

[2] Wagner, *Warfare Prayer*, pp. 61-62.

[3] Ibid, p. 62.

PART TWO

——————◆——————

PERSONAL LEVEL
THE FAMILY

"Finally, my brethren, be strong in the Lord and in the power of His might. Put on the whole armor of God, that you may be able to stand against the wiles of the devil."

(Ephesians 6:10-11)

CHAPTER FOUR

SATAN'S SCHEMES AGAINST THE FAMILY

The word scheme is from the Greek word *methodeia* (*meta*, in front of, h*odos*, path) meaning method, tactic, strategy, trick, cunning, etc.; to follow an established plan or format.

It's interesting how Paul's instructions regarding spiritual warfare in Ephesians 6:10 begin with the word "finally." Paul has been teaching the Ephesian church the importance of relationships between husband and wife, parents and children, employers and employees (or slaves and masters), and those in leadership and under authority.

> "If I understand Paul's logic, God's armor and principles of spiritual warfare are not limited to their explanation of exorcism, the occult, or the rare and exotic phenomena experienced in missionary fields. We cannot separate spiritual warfare from the events of everyday life." [1]

I believe that Satan's plan has been to destroy the three institutions established by God: the family, the church, and the nations. He accomplishes this by commanding the principalities, the ruling powers of darkness and evil spirits in high places, to war against them.

EXAMPLES FROM SCRIPTURE

As we read in the book of Genesis, from the beginning Satan's main goal has always been to destroy that which God has blessed. The first thing that God blessed in the Bible was the ordinance of marriage (Genesis 1.28). Here Satan, as father of lies, destroyer, and master of deceit, immediately looked for a way to come between God and man, between man and woman. Through lies and deceit he was able to lure the woman to disobey God and seduce the man. He then led them into a spirit of accusation in which the man blamed the woman and God, and the woman immediately accused the serpent (Satan), trying to put the blame on anyone but herself.

Once communication with God has been cut off and the relationship is broken, Satan comes onto the scene to destroy the family and the relationships between its members. In this manner, Cain was possessed by a spirit of rejection which caused anger and jealousy, leading him to kill his own brother. Later on we see Satan using fallen angels to live and procreate with the daughters of man. Through this action he brings great abomination to God's eyes (Genesis 6:1-4). " That the Sons of God saw the daughters of men, that they were beautiful; and they took wives for themselves of all whom they chose" (Genesis 6:4).

The term *"sons of God"* is always used in the context of angels, with the exception of Adam who is referred to as such in Luke 4:38. In these verses, scholars generally agree that it refers to "angels who rebelliously left heaven to take women as wives. This latter view has interpretive difficulties but seems the most likely. It also serves to reinforce the pre-flood evil in the world, for God abhors interbreeding of unlike species."[2]

The final outcome: man's heart and the intention of his thoughts became totally evil. For this reason, in the days of Noah, God was deeply afflicted in his heart and almost wiped mankind from the face of the earth. Nevertheless, he spared Noah because he was a righteous man. Then once again God "blessed" him and his family and commanded them to reproduce and fill the earth.

After the great flood, Noah got drunk and opened a door for Satan's attack. It may be that his son Ham committed a homosexual act with his drunken father, since whatever he did angered Noah to the point that he cursed Ham and his descendants. Once again, this was an attempt to destroy God's blessings by destroying family relationships.

THE MORAL DECAY OF TODAY'S GENERATION IN THE UNITED STATES HAS BEEN THE RESULT OF SATAN'S ATTEMPT TO DESTROY OUR NATION

Throughout the book of Genesis the model is the same. At Sarah's request, Abraham and Hagar engaged in an ungodly relationship. Jealousy and rejection entered the scene when Ishmael was conceived. The result was a shattered and destroyed relationship in the heart of the family.

Lot and his family were spared from the wrath of God against the wickedness of Sodom and Gomorrah, but because of his wife's disobedience, God destroyed her. Later on, his daughters, under the pretense of preserving the family, caused

Lot to get drunk and committed incest with him.

Then it was Isaac, Rebekah, and her two sons. Through a deceitful act, Jacob robbed Esau of his blessing, resulting once again in a broken family relationship. Jacob continued the destruction by deceiving Laban. Rachel stole property from her father and lied in order to cover up what she had done.

Jacob and Rachel later reaped what they had sown in their favorite son. Joseph became the target of envy, rejection, and jealousy by his own brothers. He was eventually sold and taken for dead, causing his family a great deal of pain and grief. Satan is aware that the family serves as a base for all healthy relationships. The family is the birthplace for the destiny of God.

> "First we are born into an earthly family. This is our first human relationship, or first exposure to the government. . . almost all social problems can derive from a collapse in the family. . .The church is biblically a family of families." [3]

Scripture tells us that the punishment for sin can be passed on to the fourth generation (Deuteronomy 5:9). The moral decay of today's generation in the United States has been the result of Satan's attempt to destroy our nation. He has placed evil spirits over government institutions in our nation, our cities, and our churches. "There are satanic forces over nations and communities; there are forces that influence our churches and individuals. Wherever there is a stronghold, we should realize there's an evil influence behind it. Specifically, there is a 'school of thought' which has become a dwelling place for demonic activities." [4]

The goal of Satan is to destroy the institutions of marriage and family through (1) the lust of the eyes, (2) the cravings of the flesh, (3) and the vanity of life. He is able to destroy them in the same way he has done since the beginning (1 John 2:16).

MIND-SETS OR PREDISPOSED MINDS

The term *mind-set* is a compound word that defines a mind that is set or closed to anything contrary to what it believes. It is a way of thinking that has developed over the years based on what a person has been taught, experienced, or observed from their surroundings. Mind-sets can be passed on from generation to generation through practices, rituals, beliefs, and other things that affect our society.

Satan's main attack against the believer is in the mind where our thoughts, speculations, and imaginations take place. This is why it becomes the battleground for spiritual warfare and the birthplace of all confusion and wickedness. Through deceit, Satan fills man's heart with evil and then uses it as a powerful weapon to prevent or destroy God's work.

Spirits of adultery, fornication, strife, deceit, sensuality, pride, and negligence have all been released upon the church and the nation in order to destroy the family and its roots. You can see the results in the increase of divorces, abortions, adolescent suicides, drug-related crimes, and homosexuality, including same-sex marriages. It can also be witnessed in the rapid growth of Eastern Religion, the occult, witchcraft, and the New Age movement.

BATTLING FOR OUR FAMILIES

As Nehemiah did before the restoration of the walls, we are called to evaluate the situation (consider the times) and provide men and women (families) with the necessary armor.

We must instruct them with strategies in the use of their spiritual weapons in order to take an offensive position in the battle for our families, our homes, and our Churches. We must allow God to upset the enemy's plans (see Nehemiah 4:13). Through unity we can build strong protective walls (Nehemiah 4:6).

In spiritual warfare, "resistance" takes place in the mind. The spirit of this world (our flesh or evil nature) is against the Spirit of God through the spirit that has rebelled (Romans 7:14-25). Take note of the following verses:

> "For we know that the law is spiritual, but I am carnal, sold under sin. For what I am doing, I do not understand. For what I will to do, that I do not practice, but what I hate, that I do. If then, I do what I will not to do, I agree with the law that it is good. But now, it is no longer I who do it, but sin that dwells in me. For I know that in me (that is, in my flesh) nothing good dwells, for to will is present with me, but how to perform what is good I do not find. For the good that I will to do, I do not do, but the evil I will not do that I practice. Now if I do what I will not to do, it is no longer I who do it, but sin that dwells in me. I find than a law, that evil is present with me, the one who wills to do good. For I delight in the law of God according, to the inward man. But I see another law in my members, warring against the law of my mind, and bringing me into captivity to the law of sin which is in my members. O wretched man that I am! Who will deliver me from this body of death? I thank God through Jesus Christ our Lord! So then, with the mind I myself serve the law of God, but with the flesh the law of sin." (Romans 7:14-25)

We are called to battle "aggressively" for our families: *"The Kingdom of heaven suffers violence and the violent take it by force"* (Matthew 11:12 italics added). The enemy's battle plans have not changed since the Garden of Eden. Satan came to kill, steal, and destroy families and our communion with God. But God has given us the following defensive and offensive weapons to make war against the enemy and put him under our feet:

1. The Blood of Jesus
2. The Name of Jesus
3. The Holy Spirit
4. The Word of God
5. Different kinds of prayers and fasting
6. Worship and praise
7. The ministry of angels
8. The love of God

By knowing how to use these weapons, we can successfully accomplish what Nehemiah 4:14 says: "…do not be afraid of them. Remember the Lord, great and awesome, and fight for your brethren, your sons, your daughters, your wives, and your houses."

Notes

[1] Kinnaman, p. 68.

[2] *Spirit Filled Life Bible*. Nashville TN: Thomas Nelson Publishers, 1991, p. 14.

[3] Dennis Peacock, *The Rebuilder Magazine*, April 1990, p. 3.

[4] Francis Frangipane, *The Three Battlegrounds*. Marion IA: Advancing Church Publications, 1989, p. 20.

CHAPTER FIVE

SATAN, THE DECEIVER

So the great dragon was cast out, the serpent of old, called the Devil and Satan, who deceives the whole world; he was cast to the earth, and his angels were cast out with him. (Revelation 12:9)

The Bible states that Satan is the "deceiver" who deceives the whole world. He is called the father of lies. This clearly points out that Satan has been successful in deceiving both believers and unbelievers.

Much of the controversy that has risen within the body of Christ regarding doctrinal theology, style of worship, and spiritual manifestations has arisen due to Satan's deception though what I call "philosophical strongholds." *"Beware lest anyone cheat you through philosophy and empty deceit, according to the tradition of men, according to the basic principles of the world, and not according to Christ"* (Colossians 2:8 italics added). These are also referred to as "religious strongholds," or as Dick Eastman puts it, "Satanically Inspired Beliefs."[1]

Because philosophies or ideologies are passed on through teaching or observation, it requires a receptacle, which is the mind. Because the primary area of battle is our minds, we are exhorted by the apostle Paul to put on the mind of Christ. "Let this mind be in you which was also in Christ Jesus..." (Philippians 2:5)

This passage of scripture exhorts us to have the same attitude and to focus our minds on the same things that Christ did. To accomplish this, we must begin to see all things through God's eyes. When we lose our focus from the attitude, character, and personality of Christ, we give the enemy opportunity to attack, because *"...your adversary the devil walks about like a roaring lion, seeking whom he may devour"*(1Peter 5:8 italics added).

When the enemy finds a weak spot in our Christian character, he immediately assigns spiritual powers, unclean and deceiving spirits filled with lies and deceit. The Word of God exhorts us to "resist the devil" and not give him a foothold. When the Bible speaks of the devil, it is generally referring to his kingdom, the kingdom of darkness, the rulers of this kingdom of darkness, and to the forces of wickedness in heavenly places. Satan is a liar and the father of lies. The fundamental argument is that his primary scheme is to deceive; thus, operating in the realm of lies and deception.

"Why do you not understand My speech? Because you are not able to listen to My word. You are of your father the devil, and the desires of your father you want to do. He was a murderer from the beginning, and does not stand in the truth, because there is no truth in him. When he speaks a lie, he speaks from his own resources, for he is a liar and the father of lies." (John 8:43-44)

Lucifer fell for attempting to take God's glory, and to this day he is trying to hinder the Lord from receiving any of His glory. His primary tactic is to attack the thoughts and experiences of God's children. He accomplishes this through lies, pretense, and deception.

WHEN THE ENEMY FINDS A WEAK SPOT IN OUR CHRISTIAN CHARACTER, HE IMMEDIATELY ASSIGNS SPIRITUAL POWERS, UNCLEAN AND DECEIVING SPIRITS FILLED WITH LIES AND DECEIT

During the Middle East conflict called 'Desert Storm,' the allied armies deceived the Iraqi forces by staging a naval attack, when in reality the invasion had begun in the middle of the Iraqi desert. "Deception is an effective strategy. Without going into detail about how this works in the human mind, we can say that when we are being deceived, we usually think we are in truth. This makes us susceptible to voices that speak with apparent sincerity and authority." [2] As a result, enmity and resentment creep in. This is why Paul exhorts us to use our spiritual weapons and to do the following:

"We give no offense in anything, that our ministry may not be blamed. But in all things we commend ourselves as ministers of God, in much patience, in tribulations, in needs, in distresses, in stripes, in imprisonment, in tumults, in labors, in sleeplessness, in fasting, by purity, by knowledge, by longsuffering, by kindness, by the Holy Spirit, by sincere love."
(2 Corinthians 6:3-6)

An error we easily fall into is that of ignoring the fact that we are susceptible to being deceived. That is why we must declare that the body of Christ must not be divided against itself, because a house divided against itself cannot stand. Satan deceives us when we think we don't need each other. Often we fail to understand what God is teaching us through others. By hindering the relationship between believers, Satan sets up strongholds and obstacles in the Lord's vineyard.

> "The coming of the lawless one is according to the working of Satan, with all power, signs, and lying wonders, and with all unrighteous deception among those who perish, because they did not receive the love of the truth, that they might be saved. And for this reason God will send them strong delusion, that they should believe the lie, that they all may be condemned who did not believe the truth but had pleasure in unrighteousness." (2 Thessalonians 2:9-12)

Satan is a powerful adversary, but Jesus Christ stripped him of the power he had over fear and death. The Lord delivered us from fear of an eternal death that has kept many under bondage all of their lives. The Bible offers no reference to demonic activities except in the case of the Egyptian magicians that duplicated the miracles of Moses.

Dr. Timothy M. Warner, professor of missions and director of the doctorate program at the Trinity School of Evangelical Divinity in Illinois and missionary in Sierra Leon, West Africa, wrote: "The Bible is not a book to glorify Satan or to boast about Satanic power; the Bible glorifies God in His creation and redemption. Thus, it teaches us that we must be cautious about giving too much attention to Satanic activity. Some testimonies and publications encourage us to believe in the power of Satan, giving glory to the enemy and his works and not to God."[3]

God has given the saints His power to do spiritual warfare until we put the enemy under the feet of Jesus. Yet, Satan has deceived the Body of Christ into believing that the evidence of power is something supernatural, when in reality the early Church believed that the evidence of the power of God was a natural result of the work of ministry. Dr. C. Peter Wagner says, "It is easy to fall prey to Satan's lies, especially when we lose touch with the power of God."

The apostle Paul states, "Do not be deceived, God is not mocked, whatever a man sows, that he will also reap" (Galatians 6:7 italics added), and "I have fought the good fight, I have finished the race, I have kept the faith" (2 Timothy 4:7 italics added). Remember that "pride comes before the fall," and we need to fight until we obtain the victory.

The early church knew that it was linked to an unlimited source of power. We need to confront the forces of darkness with the wisdom of God and the mind of Christ in order to fulfill the great commission. To reach the lost in these days we need power evangelism and violent confrontations with the kingdom of darkness.

Notes
[1] Dick Eastman, *Love on Its Knees*. Grand Rapids MI: Chosen Books, 1989, p. 112.

[2] C. Peter Wagner, *Wrestling with Dark Angels*. Ventura CA: Regal Books, 1990, Chapter 4.

[3] T.M. Warner, *Deception Satan's Chief Tactic*. Ventura CA: Regal Books, 1990, p. 104.

CHAPTER SIX

SPIRITUAL WARFARE IN THE BATTLEFIELD OF THE MIND

For what man knows the things of a man except the spirit of the man which is in him? Even so no one knows the things of God except the Spirit of God. Now we have received not the spirit of the world, but the Spirit who is from God, that we might know the things that have been freely given to us by God. These things we also speak, not in words which man's wisdom teaches, but which the Holy Spirit teaches, comparing spiritual things with spiritual. But the natural man does not receive the things of the Spirit of God, for they are foolishness to him, nor can he know them, because they are spiritually discerned. (1Corinthians 2:11-14)

These verses indicate there are three different types of spiritual levels that influence the decisions of an individual and will try to influence his behavior and his lifestyle. They are:

1. **Spirit of man:** it obeys the law of the mind - verse 11
2. **Spirit of God:** it obeys the law of God - verse 11
3. **Spirit of the world:** it obeys the law of sin - verse 12

THE SPIRITUAL BATTLE HAS TO BE FOUGHT IN THE SPIRITUAL REALM

"For though we walk in the flesh, we do not war according to the flesh." (2 Corinthians 10:3 italics added)

The spirit of man, or the spirit of the world, cannot understand the things of God. Other than the man himself, only God can know the thoughts and intentions of a person's heart. When the believer, a person who has been born again, receives the Spirit who comes from God, then a part of God's divine nature is imparted to man. The apostle John calls it the Spirit of Truth. God is Spirit and He has given us His Spirit to dwell within us. Man is a tripartite being consisting of spirit, soul, and body. "Now may the God of peace Himself sanctify you completely; and may your whole spirit, soul, and body be preserved blameless at the coming of our Lord Jesus Christ" (1 Thessalonians 5:23).

The natural man is spiritually dead. Because of this, every person has to be spiritually born again. If this experience of regeneration or new birth doesn't occur, his spiritual nature will remain dead. When a person is born again, God imparts to that person a new nature. He gives us His Spirit and we are born again spiritually. We are a new creation, and His Spirit dwells within us.

In the Old Testament, you cannot find the word conscience. The New Testament, however, mentions it thirty two-times. In Hebrew, it was called, 'the spirit of man' *(ruwach)*, soul, perception, reason, mind, comprehension, intelligence (Proverbs 20:27; Job 32:8; Proverbs 18:14, Ecclesiastes 7:9). The spirit of man dwells within his soul; the mind, the will, and the emotions reside in that part of man's nature. Commonly, it is known as man's conscience. The spirit of man is the lamp of the Lord that searches or scrutinizes the deep things of the heart, of one's being (Acts 24:16; John 8:9; 2 Corinthians 1:12; 1 Timothy 1:5; Hebrews 13:18; Romans 2:14,15; 9:1; 13:1,5). *"The spirit of a man is the lamp of the Lord, searching all the inner depths of his heart"* (Proverbs 20:27 italics added).

A lamp gives light; it illuminates, radiates, and reveals. "...who show the work of the law written in their hearts, their conscience also bearing witness, and between themselves their thoughts accusing or else excusing them" (Romans 2:15).

In the midst of the spiritual battle, the resistance takes place in the mind; it is the Spirit of God against the spirit of the world.

"For we know that the law is spiritual, but I am carnal, sold under sin. For what I am doing, I do not understand. For what I will to do, that I do not practice, but what I hate, that I do. If, then, I do what I will not to do, I agree with the law that it is good. But now, it is no longer I who do it, but sin that dwells in me. For I know that in me (that is, in my flesh) nothing good dwells; for to will is present with me, but how to perform what is good I do not find. For the good that I will to do, I do not do; but the evil I will not do, that I practice. Now if I do what I will not to do, it is no longer I who do it, but sin that dwells in me. I find then a law, that evil is present with me, the one who wills to do good. For I delight in the law of God according to the inward man. But I see another law in my members, warring against the law of my mind, and bringing me into captivity to the law of sin which is in my members. O wretched man that I am! Who will

deliver me from this body of death? I thank God
through Jesus Christ our Lord! So then, with the mind
I myself serve the law of God, but with the flesh the
law of sin." (Romans 7:14-25)

The battle, or spiritual conflict, between our carnal and
spiritual natures is the battle between the Spirit of God and
the spirit of the world that dwell within us. This battle always
takes place in the spirit of man, that is, in the mind, where the
will and the emotions reside. The carnal and the spiritual natures will fight in the soul. Each one will try to defeat, or
conquer and destroy, the other if the will of man permits it.
The apostle Paul delights in the law of God that dwells in the
inner man (the revealed Spirit, the Spirit of God). The fact
that the Spirit of life had freed him from the law of sin and
death made him recognize that the carnal nature fights con-
tinuously with the new spiritual nature. He recognized that
the battlefield is in the mind. It is with the mind that he served
the law of God and with the flesh he served the law of sin, of
which he was captive (verse 23).

IN THE MIDST OF THE SPIRITUAL BATTLE, THE
RESISTANCE TAKES PLACE IN THE MIND; IT IS THE
SPIRIT OF GOD AGAINST THE SPIRIT OF THE WORLD

The Holy Spirit within your own spirit tries to put your
soul, your mind, your will, your emotions, and your conscience
under submission, control, or obedience; that is, under con-
formity to the things of the Spirit, to the law of God. In other
words, you are guided, managed, or directed by the Spirit of
God, and your spirit (spirit of man) submits to the direction

and the control of the Spirit of God. At the same time, your flesh, the carnal nature in you, is also trying to guide or control your mind, your will, your emotions, and your conscience. Through your five senses (hearing, sight, touch, taste, smell), your carnal nature attacks your soul to bring it under submission or control of the flesh, that is, to obey the law of sin. Satan battles against God's nature using the flesh. Furthermore, he utilizes the five senses like instruments to motivate and control the mind to do what does not please God, that which is unpleasant and offensive to God.

"I say then: Walk in the Spirit, and you shall not fulfill the lust of the flesh. For the flesh lusts against the Spirit; and the Spirit against the flesh; and these are contrary to one another, so that you do not do the things that you wish." (Galatians 5:16-17)

"For all that is in the world, the lust of the flesh, the lust of the eyes, and the pride of life, is not of the Father but is of the world." (1 John 2:16)

Desire or lust *(epithumeo)* is the human impulse that motivates us to sin. The Christian needs to know and confess that the Spirit of God within us is more powerful than the spirit of the world. We can put our minds on the things of the Spirit of God and not on the things of the flesh and we can be guided by the Spirit of God. And yes, we can defeat the attacks of the enemy, who uses our flesh against us. Paul states that the flesh is at enmity with God. If you destroy imaginations, thoughts, and arguments that come against the obedience of Christ, the carnal nature will not be able to control you. Instead, the Spirit of God will control you (2 Corinthians 10:3-5; Romans 8:5-8, 13-14). Through covetousness (to desire anx-

iously) of the eyes, the desire of the flesh, and the pride and
arrogance of life, the spirit of man desires to control you, and
if it succeeds it will only bring you to destruction. If we live
according to the flesh, we invite death and destruction.

> "So when the woman saw that the tree was good for
> food, that it was pleasant to the eyes, and a tree desir-
> able to make one wise, she took of its fruit and ate.
> She also gave to her husband with her, and he ate."
> (Genesis 3:6)

The spirit of man consists in his will. You can follow the
direction of the flesh or of the spirit, but you cannot serve two
masters. The spiritual man looks for the things of God; his
soul desires to be satisfied by his thirst for the living God.
David wrote in Psalm 42:2a (italics added): *My soul thirsts
for God, for the living God.*

The enemy attacks man through the works of the flesh.
By way of the five senses and by the spirit of the world, the
spirit of man is confronted with arrows of jealousy, envy,
division, hate, and lust; and poverty, sickness, and physical
death are the result of embracing carnal pleasures and the things
of the world. While the enemy is attacking man, the Spirit of
God desires to give new life to the spirit of man. God asks
man to renew his mind. This new way of thinking will guide
man to put the flesh under submission and draw close to God.
The desire of the Spirit of God is to lift the level of your soul
and your body to the measure of a perfect and mature man and
to the fullness of Christ.

SPIRITUAL BATTLE IN THE FIELD OF THE MIND

THE WORD OF GOD (FAITH THROUGH HEARING)	WORLD	WORD OF SATAN (FEAR THROUGH HEARING)
Spirit of God	Spirit of man	Spirit of the World
9 manifestations (gifts) 9 characteristics (fruits) Anointing Authority	Authority Mind Will Emotions Conscience	Works of the flesh jealousy, envy, conflicts, anger, division, pride discord, hate, lasciviousness through the five senses
Spirit	Soul	Body

The fruit is produced in the spirit of man under the direction of the Holy Spirit. "By this My Father is glorified, that you bear much fruit, so you will be My disciples." (John 15:8)

Galatians chapters 5 & 6 show us the works of the flesh and the works of the Spirit. If you sow to the Spirit, you bear spiritual fruit. If you sow to the flesh, you bear carnal fruit; this prevents you from receiving the blessings of the Kingdom of God and claiming your inheritance. If you sow for the flesh, the results will be death, but if you sow for the Spirit, you receive life and peace.

1. Pneuma (spirit): You cannot sin (1 John 4:9; 1 John 5:18). The dimension of the perfect man. The fullness of Christ (Ephesians 4:13). God wishes to bring us to spiritual maturity, guided by His Spirit.

2. Psyche (soul): Ego, mind, conscience, will, emotion, intellect; "psycho": the study of the psyche.

3. Soma (body): Five senses - the dimension of the carnal man. Satan's desire is to bring us to spiritual destruction through the carnal mind and flesh.

"If you walk according to the desires of the flesh, and you put your mind on the things of the flesh, you are permitting the spirit of the world to take control of your will. When you do that, you cannot please God. But if you put your mind on the things of the Spirit and control your flesh, then you are not a slave to sin and you can enjoy life and peace."
(Galatians 5:16-26).

CHAPTER SEVEN

THE STRONGHOLD OF A HARDENED HEART

Although He had done so many signs before them, they did not believe in Him. "Therefore they could not believe, because Isaiah said again: He has blinded their eyes and hardened their hearts, lest they should see with their eyes, lest they should understand with their hearts and turn so that I should heal them." (John 12:37, 39-40)

One of the strongholds that Satan uses to destroy the people of God is to harden men's hearts. In this way, he blinds the spiritual eyes that reveal the things of God to the inner man. Unbelief, doubt, and fear prevent us from believing in the promises of God. The people of Israel provoked the wrath of God because of their unbelief. They could not enter into God's rest, or delight in His promises, even though they had witnessed the miracles that He did in the desert because the sin of unbelief had hardened their hearts - opposition to God has consequences. The words of a hardened heart give life to wicked works, and bring confusion to the Kingdom of God.

"A good man out of the good treasure of his heart brings forth good; and an evil man out of the evil treasure of his heart brings forth evil for out of the abundance of the heart his mouth speaks" (Luke 6:45).

"Therefore, as the Holy Spirit says, 'Today, if you will hear His voice, do not harden your hearts as in the rebellion, in the days of trial in the wilderness, where your fathers tested Me, tried Me, and saw My works forty years. Therefore, I was angry with that generation, and said, they always go astray in their heart, and they have not known My ways; So I swore in My wrath; they shall not enter My rest.' Beware, brethren, lest there be in any of you an evil heart of unbelief in departing from the living God; but exhort one another daily, while it is called 'Today', lest any of you be hardened through the deceitfulness of sin. For we have become partakers of Christ, if we hold the beginning of our confidence, steadfast to the end, while it is said: 'Today, if you hear His voice, do not harden your hearts as in the rebellion'. For who, having heard, rebelled? Indeed, was it not all who came out of Egypt, led by Moses? Now with whom was He angry forty years? Was it not with those who sinned, whose corpses fell in the wilderness? And to whom did He swear that they would not enter His rest, but to those who did not obey? So we see that they could not enter in because of unbelief." (Hebrews 3:7-19)

WHY OUR HEARTS BECOME HARDENED

We could see that the people didn't believe God even though they witnessed His miracles. Today's Church is the same: the majority of Christians doubt what they believe, and believe what they doubt. The moment we believe in the promises of God and begin to exercise our faith, then we start to doubt our doubts and believe our convictions. We become strengthened and can defeat the enemy (1 John 2:14). The spirits of opposition and confusion prevent God from working and contaminate the heart of man.

> "And He said, 'What comes out of man, that defiles a man. For from within, out of the heart of men proceed evil thoughts, adulteries, fornication, murders, thefts, covetousness, wickedness, deceit, lewdness, evil eye, blasphemy, pride, and foolishness. All these evil things come from within and defile a man.'" Mark 7:20-23

Satan fills man's heart with wickedness and deception. "And Jesus answered and said to them: 'Take heed that no one deceives you. For many will come in My name, saying, I am the Christ, and will deceive many'" (Matthew 24:4-5).

IN TODAY'S CHURCH, THE MAJORITY OF
CHRISTIANS DOUBT WHAT THEY BELIEVE,
AND BELIEVE WHAT THEY DOUBT

The predisposed mind is a stronghold to destroy and obstruct the work of God. This mindset hardens the heart and prevents us from seeing the things of God. The Pharisees, blinded by traditions, couldn't see the promised Messiah, the liberator of Israel, because of their mental predisposition of how and when the liberator would come. "...but exhort one another daily while it is called, 'Today,' lest any of you be hardened through the deceitfulness of sin" (Hebrews 3:13).

The unleashed spirits against the family are the following: adultery, fornication, covetousness, deceit, sensuality, arrogance, pride, and rebellion.

The main source of conflict in relationships between Christians and in the family comes from selfish desires that become more important than the will of God. The desire to be recognized and honored and the desire for power and money causes the hardening of our hearts and prevents us from seeing the glory of God.

HEALTHY RELATIONSHIPS

The apostle Paul exhorts the church in Ephesus on healthy relationships:

Husbands and Wives

"Wives, submit to your own husbands, as to the Lord. For the husband is head of the wife, as also Christ is head of the church; and He is the Savior of the body."   (Ephesians 5:22-23)

Parents and Children

"Children, obey your parents in the Lord, for this is right. Honor your father and mother, which is the first commandment with a promise, that it may be well with you and you may live long on the earth." And you fathers, do not provoke your children to wrath, but bring them up in the training and admonition of the Lord."   (Ephesians 6:1-4)

Masters and Bondservants

"Bondservants, be obedient to those who are your masters according to the flesh, with fear and trembling, in sincerity of heart, as to Christ, not with eye service, as men pleasers, but as bondservants of Christ, doing the will of God from the heart, with good will doing service, as to the Lord, and not to men, knowing that whatever good anyone does, he will receive the same from the Lord, whether he is a slave or free. And you, masters, do the same things to them, giving up threatening, knowing that your own Master also is in heaven, and there is no partiality with Him" (Ephesians 6:5-9).

The direction that Paul takes is to be strong *(enduamoo)* in the Lord and in the strength of His power *(ischus)*. "Finally, my brethren be strong in the Lord, and in the power of His might" (Ephesians 6:10). "..and what is the exceeding greatness of His power toward us who believe, according to the working of His mighty power" (Ephesians 1:19).

In his book *Overcoming the Dominion of Darkness*, Gary Kinnaman says, "The foundations for spiritual warfare are not limited to exorcism, occult practices, etc. We cannot disconnect spiritual warfare from the daily affairs of our lives." [1]

In America and the Western world we have seen a substantial increase in divorce, adultery, and fornication resulting in pregnancies and abortions among adolescents. Common law arrangements, homosexuality, lesbianism, and moral decay are destroying the fiber of society and family relations. This is prevalent in the world of unbelievers, but lately it is growing roots and increasing within the Church and within its leadership. We cannot rebuild the church and restore Zion until we confront the attacks of the enemy and the battle that has been waged against the family.

Nehemiah talked to the nobles (elders, leaders, etc.), the authorities (employees and volunteers), and the rest of the people (church congregation), encouraging them to remember how great and powerful God is and to fight (battle, war, etc.) for their brothers, for their children and wives (families), and for their homes.

"Therefore, I positioned men behind the lower parts of the wall, at the openings; and I set the people according to their families, with their swords, their spears, and their bows. And I looked and arose and said to the nobles, to the leaders, and to the rest of the people, "do not be afraid of them. Remember the Lord, great and awesome, and fight for your brethren, your sons, your daughters, your wives, and your houses." (Nehemiah 4:13-14)

GOD'S PLAN FOR REDEEMING RELATIONSHIPS

We are called to consider and observe the situations and to place men and women of God in strategic places. As a Christian family, we should equip ourselves with spiritual weapons to take the offensive in the battle for our families, our homes, our churches, and to permit God to hinder and obstruct the plans of the enemy.

Joshua instructs us to serve the Lord with integrity and truth. *"But as for me and my house, we will serve the Lord."* (Joshua 24:15 italics added)

Since the creation God has worked through the family to carry out His divine purposes, specifically in the area of relationships. Immediately after the creation, God gave Adam a helper in Eve and established the family unit. Before long, Satan came to cause division between them. God's patterns are not established in individualism, but in relationships and within the concept of the family.

To Adam and Eve he said: *"Be fruitful, and multiply, and replenish the earth, and subdue it"* (Genesis 1:28b italics added). And God gave them dominion. Satan came to destroy the union between Adam and Eve and the family relationship in the home. One result was Cain's murder of his brother Abel. God's redemptive plan always included the family concept and the protection of the family, but before the judgment, He took the necessary steps to retain and preserve the family patterns. When men's wickedness multiplied on the earth, God destroyed all things with a universal flood. To rebuild, God brought the animals, two by two, that is by families:

"And behold, I Myself am bringing flood waters on the earth, to destroy from under heaven all flesh in which is the breath of life; everything that is on the earth shall die. But I will establish My covenant with you, and you shall go into the ark, you, your sons, your wife, and your sons' wives with you. Then the lord said to Noah, 'Come into the ark, you and all your household, because I have seen that you are righteous before me in this generation'" (Genesis 6:17,18; 7:1).

In the destruction of Sodom and Gomorrah:

"Then the men said to Lot, 'Have you anyone else here? Sons-in-law, your sons, your daughters, and whomever you have in the city, take them out of this place. For we will destroy this place, because the outcry against them has grown great before the face of the Lord, and the Lord has sent us to destroy it.' So Lot went out and spoke to his sons-in-law, who had married his daughters, and said 'Get up, get out of this place; for the Lord will destroy this city!' But to his sons-in-law he seemed to be joking. When the morning dawned, the angels urged Lot to hurry, saying, 'Arise, take your wife and your two daughters who are here, lest you be consumed in the punishment of the city'" (Genesis 19:12-15).

Satan's plan is to destroy the unity and relationships between brothers as he did with Cain and Abel, between fathers and children, and within the Body of Christ through the following:

1. **The spirit of accusation (religious spirit):**
   "Then the man said, 'The woman whom you gave to be with me, she gave me of the tree, and I ate.' And the Lord God said to the woman, 'What is this you have done?' The woman said, 'The serpent deceived me, and I ate'" (Genesis 3:12-13).
2. **The spirit of rejection (can lead to murder):**
   "And in the process of time it came to pass that Cain brought an offering of the fruit of the ground to the Lord. Abel also brought of the first born of his flock and of their fat. And the Lord respected Abel and his offering, but He did not respect Cain and his offering. And Cain was very angry, and his countenance fell" (Genesis 4:3-5).

The Word of God exhorts us to purify our hearts by drawing near to God. We should believe in His promises and quit being double minded. We should exercise our faith through prayer, depositing in our hearts the treasure of his promises, for he says: "But He gives more grace therefore He says: 'God resists the proud, but gives grace to the humble.' Therefore submit to God. Resist the devil and he will flee from you." (James 4:6-7)

How do we fight back against these strongholds of the enemy? We do so by the overcoming power of God's *agape* love. The apostle Paul elaborates on the absolute necessity of love in 1 Corinthians 13. Love endures all things and never fails. The Holy Spirit inspired Paul to write about the endurance of faith, hope, and love, and concludes by stating "but the greatest of these is love" (1 Corinthians 13:14).

Notes
[1] Kinnaman, p. 68.

PART THREE

SPIRITUAL LEVEL
THE CHURCH

"And I also say to you that you are Peter, and on this rock I will build My church, and the gates of Hades shall not prevail against it."

(Matthew 16:18)

CHAPTER EIGHT

SPIRITS UNLEASHED AGAINST THE CHURCH

Now the Spirit expressly says that in latter times some will depart from the faith, giving heed to deceiving spirits and doctrines of demons, speaking lies in hypocrisy, having their own conscience seared with a hot iron (1 Timothy 4:1-2).

Satan is the master of deceit. Part of his strategy is to infiltrate the church causing division, discouragement, immorality, and the promotion of false ideologies. To a certain degree, his objectives are reached by assigning lying and accusing spirits that hinder the spiritual and numeric growths of local churches.

In this section we will study the characteristics of lying and hypocritical spirits. Generally these spirits bring lies in the form of accusations, false doctrines, manipulation, and many others. It is important to make clear that when we use the term 'spirit' we are not simply referring to a supernatural being, ghost, or angel. W.E. Vine's *The Expository Dictionary of New Testament Words*[1] defines the term *pneuma* as "the sensitive element in man, that through which he can receive, reflect, feel, or desire." (Matthew 5:3; 26:41; Acts 17:16; 2 Corinthians 7:1). A "spirit" can be defined as a mental predisposition, a mind-set, or a state of being, thus facilitating our understanding of the terms spirit of bitterness, wrath, jealousy, envy, drunkenness, etc. (see tables 1 and 2 in chapter 10).

In this chapter, we will be discussing some of the most devastating spirits unleashed against the Church.

THE SPIRIT OF ANTICHRIST

"Little children, it is the last hour and as you have heard that the Antichrist is coming, even now many antichrists have come by which we know that it is the last hour. They went out from us, but they were not of us; for if they had been of us, they would have continued with us; but they went out that they might be made manifest, that none of them were of us." (1 John 2:18,19)

The prefix "anti" does not mean "against." In biblical terms it refers to "instead of," vs. one or many who profess to be "Christs," redeemers, or saviors - those that deceive through false and deceiving doctrines. This spirit invaded the early Church and caused division. We, therefore, cannot limit our understanding of this spirit as a person that shall come in the future. The apostle John says that many antichrists have surfaced and they cause division among the church. "They went out from us... they would have continued with us, but they went out... none of them were of us" (1 John 2:19).

Almost every congregation, especially the older ones, has been the victim of individuals controlled by this divisive spirit which has broken the unity of the faith and fueled rebellion. "..and every spirit that does not confess that Jesus Christ has come in the flesh is not of God. And this is the spirit of the Antichrist, which you have heard was coming, and is now already in the world" (1 John 4:3). "To confess Jesus is more than just mentioning His name in prayer. It means to be in unity with Him."[2]

ALMOST EVERY CONGREGATION HAS
BEEN THE VICTIM OF INDIVIDUALS
CONTROLLED BY A DIVISIVE SPIRIT

The spirit of antichrist hardens the heart, keeping it untouched by love. This spirit nourishes wrong attitudes like unforgiveness; it causes the unity of the faith in Jesus to be fragmented and divided due to criticism and doctrinal differences that are unimportant. It embraces the lack of forgiveness and promotes division and hate, instead of forgiveness, unity, and love. This spirit fuels rebellion and especially opposes truth. It is an independent spirit that promotes the individual and embraces denominationalism, independence, and opposes reconciliation.

"...who opposes and exalts himself above all that is called God or that is worshipped, so that he sits as God in the temple of God, showing himself that he is God." (2 Thessalonians 2:4)

THE SPIRIT OF ABSALOM

The majority of pastors have, at one time or another, been confronted with someone similar to David's son. This is an independent spirit which refuses to submit to authorities anointed by God. They usurp authority, inciting others to rebel and to replace the authority ordained by God. Absalom allowed a root of bitterness to control his life. He found out that his half brother, Amnon (David's son), had raped and despised his sister, Tamar. From that very day, Absalom carefully planned his revenge. From this we can see a spirit of revenge and hate which premeditated a crime of vengeance.

"And Absalom her brother said to her, 'Has Amnon your brother been with you? But now hold your peace, my sister, he is your brother; do not take this thing to heart.' So Tamar remained desolate in her brother Absalom's house. But when King David heard of all these things, he was very angry. And Absalom spoke to his brother Amnon neither good nor bad, for Absalom hated Amnon, because he had forced his sister Tamar. ...Now Absalom had commanded his servants, saying, 'Watch now, when Amnon's heart is merry with wine, and when I say to you, 'Strike Amnon!' then kill him. Do not be afraid. Have I not commanded you? Be courageous and valiant.'"
(2 Samuel 13:20-22, 28)

"Then Jonadab the son of Shimeah, David's brother, answered and said, 'Let not my lord suppose they have killed all the young men, the king's sons, for only Amnon is dead. For by the command of Absalom this has been determined from the day that he forced his sister Tamar.'" (2 Samuel 13:32)

After this incident, Absalom fled. He went to Gesur for three years until his father, David, sent for him because he missed him. When Absalom returned, he formed a group of those who were against the king. He began to give advice and pose as a counselor to those who came to his father, promising them that if he would be judge, their problems would be solved. With great diplomacy he kissed them and stole the hearts of the people of Israel.

The Bible says that Absalom was praised for his good looks; that he was perfect from the top of his head to the bottom of his feet; and that he was manipulative, proud, and vengeful. The Bible also states that Absalom built a pillar to himself in the Kings Valley because he wanted to be remembered. *"I have no son to keep my name in remembrance"* (2 Samuel 18:18b italics added). Yet we read in 2 Samuel 14:27, "To Absalom were born three sons, and one daughter whose name was Tamar."

> "Now Absalom would rise early and stand beside the way to the gate. So it was, whenever anyone who had a lawsuit came to the king for a decision, that Absalom would call to him and say, 'What city are you from?' And he would say, 'Your servant is from such and such a tribe of Israel.' Then Absalom would say to him, 'Look, your case is good and right; but there is no deputy of the king to hear you.' Moreover Absalom would say, 'Oh that I were made judge in the land, and everyone who has any suit or cause would come to me; then I would give him justice.' And so it was, whenever anyone came near to bow down to him, that he would put out his hand and take him and kiss him. In this manner Absalom acted toward all Israel who came to the king for judgment. So Absalom stole the

hearts of the men of Israel." (2 Samuel 15:2-6)

God has given us authority over the things we love. If love is not present, authority does not function. Love is always willing to pay a price, even self-denial or death. Jesus died because He loved. This redeeming love is what gives origin to authority. Absalom stole the people's hearts by pretending to love them, thus replacing God-ordained authority with rebellion. Obedience responds better and stronger to love than to fear, therefore, it must be earned.

In spite of all Absalom's schemes, lies, and apparent victories, almighty God returned David to his rightful throne and Absalom died at the hand of David's army. Every pastor, as overseer of the congregation he loves, will be defended and sustained by God, even when those with the spirit of Absalom arise against him. Those with this spirit come to cause mistrust, incite rebellion, and create division in the Kingdom of God.

"Obey those who rule over you, and be submissive, for they watch out for your souls, as those who must give account. Let them do so with joy and not with grief, for that would be unprofitable for you."
(Hebrews 13:17)

Frequently, young people are novices in the things of God, particularly those who lack biblical or theological foundations, but they have a zeal for God. Since this zeal is void of knowledge, a spirit of Absalom comes in and controls them. They don't have the patience to wait on God's timing or the wisdom to recognize it. They frequently arise against their leaders, even as Absalom arose against his father.

THE SPIRIT OF SLUMBER AND LETHARGY

"Just as it is written: 'God has given them a spirit of stupor, eyes that they should not see and ears that they should not hear, to this very day.'"   (Romans 11:8)

Webster's Dictionary defines stupor as "A state in which the mind and senses are dulled; loss of sensibility." This indifference or lethargy causes ignorance and discouragement in Christians that hinders them from growing in Christ and keeps them blinded to God's vision. It is similar to entering into a deep sleep that prevents us from serving the Lord.

Frequently a new believer is full of zeal for the things of God. He is full of excitement, witnesses, testifies, is a servant, etc., yet, if every Christian is not properly discipled, motivated, and equipped, he will soon face a state of indifference or apathy which discourages him from serving the Lord. These eventually become as the burnt stones on the wall and in God's temple (see Nehemiah 4:2).

Every pastor should do what Nehemiah did when he had the vision to rebuild the wall and returned to Jerusalem to accomplish that vision. Nehemiah personally examined the walls (members) of Jerusalem that were broken down (disheartened, discouraged) and its gates (leaders) that were burned with fire (Nehemiah 2:12-15). After Nehemiah examined the wall, he realized that he could not rebuild the wall by himself, so he challenged the people and they responded by saying, *"Let us rise up and build. Then they set their hands to this good work"* (Nehemiah 2:18b italics added).

Ministry is the work of the saints; that is to say, of all Christians. The call to pastors and leaders is to equip the saints for the work of ministry. The results will be amazing, just as they were for Nehemiah. "So we built the wall, and the entire wall was joined together up to half its height, for the people had a mind to work" (Nehemiah 4:6).

The spirit of slumber, stupor, and lethargy particularly attacks those Christians who have not been active in ministry and who have not known the ways of the Lord for many years. They enter into a luke-warmness, such as was experienced by the church in Laodicea, of which Jesus said, *"... because you are lukewarm, and neither cold nor hot, I will vomit you out of my mouth"* (Revelation 3:16 italics added). The Church body needs to pray against this spirit so that indifference will be bound and a spirit of servanthood will be released in its place. God's people honor Him with their lips, but their hearts are far from Him. They are simply worshipping Him from memorized religious tradition. When this happens, God allows a spirit of deep sleep, known also as a spirit of slumber, to fall upon them.

Other distinctive spirits that come against the local church, such as the stronghold of "cold love" and the spirit of Jezebel, will be discussed in detail in the following chapters.

Notes

[1] WE. Vine, *The Expository Dictionary of New Testament Words.* Fleming H Revell, 1940.

[2] Frangipane, p. 92.

CHAPTER NINE

———◆———

THE OVERCOMING POWER OF LOVE

God's love is an unconditional, self-giving love. Love gives. The proof of love is reflected by the measure of the sacrifice a person is willing to make for another. *"For God so loved the world that He gave His only begotten Son, that whoever believes in Him should not perish but have everlasting life."* (John 3:16 italics added)

In Galatians 2:20, the apostle Paul states that the Son of God loved us and gave himself for us; Christ loved the church and gave Himself for it.

"Beloved, let us love one another, for love is of God; and everyone who loves is born of God and knows God. He who does not love does not know God, for God is love. In this the love of God was manifested toward us, that God has sent His only begotten Son into the world, that we might live through Him. In this is love, not that we loved God, but that He loved us and sent His Son to be the propitiation for our sins.

Beloved, if God so loved us, we also ought to love one another. No one has seen God at any time. If we love one another, God abides in us, and His love has been perfected in us." (I John 4:7-12)

As Christians, we should ask ourselves these questions: What type of love do we have in our hearts today? Is it tender love? Is it a love that is open, visible, and bright? Or is it a calculating and discriminating type of love? Is this love less vulnerable or cold?

THE SIGNS OF THE END TIMES

Jesus told his disciples the signs of the end times: "And then many will be offended, will betray one another and will hate one another. Then many false prophets will rise up and deceive many. And because lawlessness will abound, the love of many will grow cold. But he who endures to the end will be saved" (Matthew 24:10-13).

I want to address the stronghold that says, "... due to lawlessness the love of many will grow cold" (Matthew 24:12). Relationships within the Body of Christ are most prone to the attack of the enemy. One of the signs of a triumphant and unified church is its commitment to love. Due to the increase of wickedness and the enemy's deceit, Christian love is suffering terrible attacks, thereby hindering the work of God and the vision He has given us. If there is no love, there can be no unity in the Spirit, no lasting victory. Victories may come, but are soon followed by defeats. Cold love is a demonic stronghold, and "the scripture warns that in an individual's life, a small root of bitterness will defile many." [1] "...looking carefully lest anyone fall short of the grace of God; lest any root of bitterness springing up cause trouble and by this many become defiled" (Hebrews 12:15).

It is inevitable that at one time or another we may offend and hurt each other through words or deeds. After all, we do live in a complex world with different social, economical, and cultural levels. If we fail to react in love and forgiveness and hide a root of bitterness within our spirit, that bitterness, that pain, that debt will hinder us from loving and praying effectively. This will bring us to be among the many whose love grew cold mentioned in Matthew 24:12.

"But I say to you, love your enemies, bless those who curse you, do good to those who hate you, and pray for those who spitefully use you and persecute you." (Matthew 5:44)

"Confess your trespasses to one another, and pray for one another, that you may be healed. The effective, fervent prayer of a righteous man avails much." (James 5:16)

God often allows painful experiences to touch our lives to teach us to **forgive**, **love** and **pray** for those who offend us. God gives us opportunity to grow in divine love. "But God demonstrates His own love toward us, in that while we were still sinners, Christ died for us" (Romans 5:8).

For true love to exist there needs to be commitment to enter into covenant relationships. People withdraw from their commitments and covenants because their love (agape) has grown cold due to hurts and offenses.

Jesus said that in this world we would have stumbling blocks, referring to those things that cause us to stumble and fall into the enemy's traps of bitterness, anger, and unforgiveness. There are times in our lives when well-meaning people, servants of God, are experiencing a "bad" day and may offend or hurt us. This will cause us to stumble if we are quick to find offense and fail to forgive. It's no wonder Jesus rebuked the Pharisees.

ONE OF THE SIGNS OF A TRIUMPHANT AND UNIFIED CHURCH IS ITS COMMITMENT TO LOVE

Let's ask ourselves sincerely, "Have we stumbled in our Christian walk because someone has sinned against us and offended us? Has that wound caused us to distance ourselves and not show the love we used to? Have we maintained the same level of commitment with God, the Church, and the body, in spite of offenses and stumbling blocks? Negative attitudes can harden our hearts and deaden our love and commitment. Scripture is very clear on this, *"..he who loves God, must also love his brother...."* (1 John 4:21 italics added).

Love is not demonstrated with words but with actions. When we love someone, we commit ourselves, as in the marriage covenant, to remain true to that love no matter what may happen down the road. It is necessary to love each other, even with our imperfections. No one is perfect, no one is void of faults, no one is sinless; therefore, we cannot allow the enemy to make these trivialities seem as big problems due to small faults or human weaknesses. This will only deaden our love for God. "Jesus said to him, 'You shall love the Lord your God with all your heart, with all your soul, and with all your mind.'...And the second is like it; 'You shall love your neighbor as yourself'" (Matthew 22:37, 39).

Let's reflect and examine our hearts. The objective of the stronghold of a love grown cold is to make sure that the Body of Christ is divided. The adversary knows that a house divided has a weak and unstable foundation. It is a challenge to love as God loves. If we persevere we can obtain His vision and truly be imitators of Christ. No one can reach the fullness of the kingdom of God on earth without being committed to imperfect people somewhere down the road. We are an imperfect people, living in an imperfect world, and only God's perfect love will enable us to press on towards the mark of the high calling of Christ.

Notes
[1] Frangipane, p. 50.

CHAPTER TEN

———◆———

THE SPIRIT OF JEZEBEL

Nevertheless, I have a few things against you because you allow that woman, Jezebel, who calls herself a prophetess, to teach and seduce My servants to commit sexual immorality and eat things sacrificed to idols. And I gave her time to repent of her sexual immorality, and she did not repent (Revelation 2:20-21).

God continues to instruct us on how to prepare for spiritual warfare. In the city of Mesa, AZ where I formerly pastored, we had identified the strongholds of that community. Among them was the spirit of religion that produces accusation, rejection, and division. This spirit may also be called the spirit of antichrist, since it gives rise to division among the church instead of unity. Others are the spirit of stupor (laziness, recreation, and indifference) and the spirit of witchcraft (occult, drugs, and idolatry).

Satan has unleashed and assigned principalities and powers to bring division to the local church. These same spirits, in addition to the spirit of Jezebel (independence, ambition, preeminence and control) and the spirits of carnal sensuality (lasciviousness, lust, adultery and fornication) have been assigned to local churches to cause division, jealousy, and envy, and to hinder the development of God's plans and purposes. Many have been disheartened and have fallen victim to the enemy's lies due to these foul spirits. The word of God exhorts us to resist the devil and to stand firm in our faithfulness to God and the ministry to which He has called us.

> "Be sober, be vigilant, because your adversary the devil walks about like a roaring lion, seeking whom he may devour. Resist him steadfast in the faith, knowing that the same sufferings are experienced by your brotherhood in the world." (1 Peter 5:8-9)

> "You therefore, beloved, since you know this beforehand, beware lest you also fall from your own steadfastness being led away with the error of the wicked." (2 Peter 3:17)

THE SPIRIT OF JEZEBEL IS A VERY INDEPENDENT SPIRIT, ALWAYS SEEKING RECOGNITION, STATUS, AND CONTROL

> "But the heavens and the earth which are now preserved by the same word, are reserved for fire until the day of judgement and perdition of ungodly men." (2 Peter 3:7)

We need "foreknowledge" so that we may know our spiritual enemy. The only way to know the enemy is through the Word of God that teaches us that "the people perish for lack of knowledge." When we know the truth, the truth will set us free. This is why we are instructed to ... "put on the whole armor of God. In doing so, we may stand firm against the wiles of the enemy" (Ephesians 6:11).

> "Now the Spirit expressly says that in latter times some will depart from the faith, giving heed to deceiving spirits and doctrines of demons, speaking lies in hypocrisy, having their own conscience seared with a hot iron."   (1 Timothy 4:1-2)

THE ORIGIN OF THE JEZEBEL SPIRIT

What characterizes these strongholds (deceptive spirits, lying spirits, spirit of Jezebel, and religious spirits) is that they are full of hypocrisy and they speak lies because their consciences are seared. We know that Satan, the devil, is the father of lies. That is to say, every lie, every falsehood, every deception proceeds from the seed of its father, Satan.

To know the spirit of Jezebel, we need to understand its origin. We find the first mention of this name in the manipulative and rebellious wife of King Ahab.

> "In the thirty-eighth year of Asa king of Judah, Ahab the son of Omri became king over Israel; and Ahab the son of Omri reigned over Israel in Samaria twenty-two years. Now Ahab the son of Omri did evil in the sight of the Lord, more than all who were before him. And it came to pass, as though it had been a trivial thing for him to walk in the sins of Jeroboam the son

of Nebat, that he took as wife Jezebel the daughter of
Ethbaal king of the Sidonians, and he went and served
Baal and worshipped him." (1Kings 16:29-31)

"But there was no one like Ahab who sold himself to do
wickedness in the sight of the Lord, because Jezebel his wife
stirred him up" (1 Kings 21:25). It was through the manipulative spirit in Queen Jezebel that all of Israel was
contaminated. Jezebel was a native of Sidon, the capital of
Phoenicia, which was the birthplace or center of Baal worship. The main temple of Baal, the sun god, was in the city of
Tyre where fertility was worshipped. Baal took on different
names in various places, and along with him would be seen
other minor gods, such as Dagon and Ashtoreth, which are
also mentioned in the Bible. Worship to Ashtoreth, better
known as the "Queen of Heaven," included all types of pros-
titution, sexual depravity, and human sacrifice. Jezebel was
brought up in this idolatrous culture; therefore, she had deeply
rooted in her the spirits of hypocrisy, falsehood, deceit, lust,
etc.
     "The spirit of Jezebel is a very independent spirit, always
seeking recognition, status, and control. The name Jezebel
means 'without cohabitation,' which means "refuses to live
with anyone." The Word tells us, "Behold how good and pleasant it is for brethren to dwell together (cohabit) in unity."
Because the spirit of Jezebel is independent, it does not submit to authority and brings division instead of unity. It is a
spirit that wants to control and dominate in relationships. It
only submits when there is an advantage or to gain a foothold.
This spirit is not exclusive to women, although it is attracted
to the female psyche due to its ability to manipulate with
subtlety and without force. It especially attacks embittered
women who have been rejected, abandoned, or abused by men.

This spirit operates through those who desire to control others with jealousy, insecurity, and vanity. It is evident in women who publicly humiliate their husbands or try to control and manipulate them or their children by keeping them within her control in her 'nest.'" [1]

"And Ahab told Jezebel all that Elijah had done, also how he had executed all the prophets with the sword. Then Jezebel sent a messenger to Elijah, saying, 'So let the gods do to me, and more also, if I do not make your life as the life of one of them by tomorrow about this time.'"   (1 Kings 19:1-2)

"Then Jezebel his wife said to him, 'You now exercise authority over Israel! Arise, eat food, and let your heart be cheerful; I will give you the vineyard of Naboth the Jezreelite.' And she wrote letters in Ahab's name, sealed them with his seal, and sent the letters to the elders and the nobles who were dwelling in the city with Naboth. She wrote in the letters, saying, 'Proclaim a fast, and seat Naboth with high honor among the people; and seat two men, scoundrels, before him to bear witness against him, saying, 'You have blasphemed God and the king. Then take him out, and stone him, that he may die.' ...Then they took him outside the city and stoned him with stones, so that he died. Then they sent to Jezebel, saying, 'Naboth has been stoned and is dead'. And it came to pass, when Jezebel heard that Naboth had been stoned and was dead, that Jezebel said to Ahab, 'Arise, take possession of the vineyard of Naboth the Jezreelite, which he refused to give you for money; for Naboth is not alive, but dead'. ...Then the Word of the Lord came to Elijah the Tishbite, saying, 'Arise, go down to meet Ahab king of Israel, who lives in Samaria. There he is, in the vineyard of Naboth, where he has gone down to take possession of it. You shall speak to him, saying, ' Thus says the Lord: Have you murdered and also taken possession?' And you shall speak to him saying, ' Thus says the Lord: In the place where dogs licked the blood of Naboth, dogs shall lick your blood, even yours.' So Ahab said to Elijah, 'Have you found me, O my enemy?' And he answered, 'I have found you, because you have sold yourself to do evil in the sight of the Lord. ... And concerning Jezebel the Lord also spoke, saying, 'The dogs shall eat Jezebel by the wall of Jezreel. The dogs shall eat whoever belongs to Ahab and dies in the city, and the birds of the air shall eat whoever dies in the field.' But there was no one like Ahab who sold himself to do wickedness in the sight of the Lord, because Jezebel his wife stirred him up." (1 Kings 21:5-10, 13-15, 17-20, 23-25)

HOW THE SPIRIT OF JEZEBEL AFFECTS CHURCHES

Scripture tells us that Ahab was manipulated and controlled by false prophetic spirits and lying spirits that led him to rule his kingdom through deception and flattery. When God's prophets, Elijah and Micah, brought messages of discipline and correction, Ahab refused to listen.

The spirit of Jezebel manipulates husbands, wives, sons, daughters, new believers, etc. It operates through insecurity, envy, vanity, and matriarchal function. We need to beware when a woman, though used prophetically, insists on recognition and ignores and manipulates the masculine leadership of the church, calling herself a prophetess. Jezebel hates the ministry of the prophets because they expose her. This is why the prophet Elijah became her worst enemy. "When she fights, it is to put the people against the prophetic message. She hates the spoken word of God. Her real enemy is God's spoken Word." [2]

"The Spirit of Jezebel hates humility and it refuses to submit to other ministries. A genuine ministry desires to responsibly submit to other ministries." [3]. Unless those called to minister are submitted to a covering of authority, you can argue that there is an influence of the spirit of Jezebel.

During a ministry trip to Uruguay in 1992, I found that pastors in the city of Young were confused due to a Christian woman who would go from church to church trying to manipulate the pastors. She would arrive with an attitude of submission and would get involved in the work of ministry. Shortly thereafter, she would begin to prophesy and insisted on being recognized as a prophetess. She would then visit individual church members at their homes and prophesy over them, sowing seeds of division and unhappiness, thus gaining control over the feeble minded. The local pastors did not know what to do.

During the workshops on 'spiritual warfare,' the pastors realized they were dealing with the spirit of Jezebel. United in prayer the pastors broke the stronghold of Jezebel over this woman. The next day at an evangelistic crusade, through the prayer of faith, authority was taken over this spirit and the woman was set free. She recognized the spirit within her, repented, and was delivered from Satan's power.

Notes

[1] Frangipane, p.98.
[2] Ibid, p.103.
[3] Ibid, p.102.

TABLE I
SPIRITS UNLEASHED AGAINST THE CHURCH

Deceptive Spirits — 1 Timothy 4:1
Deaf and Dumb Spirit — Mark 9:17; 9:25
Spirits in Prisons (due to disobedience) — 1 Peter 3:19
Unclean Spirit — Zechariah 13:2, Mark 9:25, Rev 18:2
Spirits of Infirmity — Luke 13:11
Spirit of Jezebel — Revelations 2:20
Spirit of Man — 1 Corinthians 2:12
Spirit of Jealousy — Numbers 5:14; 5:30
Different Spirits — 2 Corinthians 11:4
Evil Spirits — 1 Samuel 16:14-23; 18:10
Spirit of Unbelief — Hebrews 3:12
Lying Spirits — 1 King 22:23, 2 Chronicles 18:21-22
Spirit of Bondage (slavery) — Romans 8:15
Spirit of Fear — 2 Timothy 1:7
Foul Spirits — Matthew 10:1;12:43, Mark 1:23,27; 1:26; 3:30; 5:2; 5:8, Luke 11:24; 8:29; 9:42, Acts 5:16;8:7; Mark 11:24
Spirit of division (evil) — Judges 9:23
Spirit of the world — 1Corinthians 2:11
Medium spirits (occultism) — 1Samuel 28:7,9
Prince of the power of the air — Ephesians 2:2
Spirits of Death — Leviticus 20:27
Spirit of Antichrist — 1John 4:3
Spirit of Idolatry (Egyptians, religious) — Leviticus 20:27
Spirit of Divination (occultism) — Acts 16:16
Ghost Spirits — Isaiah 29:4
Spirit of Error (religious) — 1 John 4:6
Spirits of Perversion (distortion) — Isaiah 19:14
Spirit of Lethargy and Stupor — Romans 11:8, Isaiah 29:10

TABLE II

SPIRITS THAT HAVE BEEN GIVEN TO COUNTERATTACK THE ENEMY'S ASSAULT

Spirit of God

Spirit of His Son

Spirit of Christ

Spirit of Faith — Corinthians 4:13

Spirit of Life — Revelations 11:11

Spirit of Adoption — Romans 8:15

Spirit of Glory — 1 Peter 4:14

Spirit of Grace — Hebrews 10:29, Zacaraiah 12:12, Isaiah 57:15

Spirit of Meekness — Corinthians 4:21, Galations 6:1

Spirit of Promise — Ephesians 1:13

Spirit of Knowledge – Isaiah 11:2

Spirit of Truth — John 14:17; 15:26; 16:13; 1John 4:6

Spirit of Wisdom — Isaiah 11:2

Spirit of Elijah — 2 Kings 2:15

Spirit of Justice — Isaiah 4:4

PART FOUR

◆

TERRITORIAL LEVEL
THE NATIONS

"But even if our gospel is veiled, it is
veiled to those who are perishing, whose
minds the god of this age has blinded,
who do not believe, lest the light of the
gospel of the glory of Christ, who is the
image of God, should shine on them."
(2 Corinthians 4:3-4)

CHAPTER ELEVEN

WHAT IS SPIRITUAL MAPPING?

I do not cease to give thanks for you, making mention of you in my prayers: That the God of our Lord Jesus Christ, the Father of glory, may give to you the spirit of wisdom and revelation in the knowledge of Him, the eyes of your understanding being enlightened; that you may know what is the hope of His calling, what are the riches of the glory of His inheritance in the saints, and what is the exceeding greatness of His power toward us who believe, according to the working of His mighty power (Ephesians 1: 16-19).

"…and He changes the times and the seasons; He removes kings and raises up kings, He gives wisdom to the wise and knowledge to those who have understanding. He reveals deep and secret things; He knows what is in the darkness and light dwells with Him."
(Daniel 2:21-22)

DEFINITIONS OF SPIRITUAL MAPPING

Though the term *'spiritual mapping'* has numerous definitions, the general consensus is that it is a new and powerful way to observe the deep forces that operate daily in the life and experiences of cities and nations. George Otis, Jr., author of the book *Last of the Giants*, a member of the Sentinel Group, and director of the investigative team of 'AD 2000,' is perhaps the most knowledgeable person on this subject matter. He defines spiritual mapping as follows: "Spiritual mapping is the means by which we take our understanding of spiritual forces and activity and apply it to places and circumstances in the natural (physical) realm." [1]

While spiritual mapping does not manipulate circumstances or the surrounding reality of events, it does help us identify the hidden causes of events that surround us and are undetectable to the natural or physical eye.

Cindy Jacobs, a special friend and partner in ministry, is a member of the 'Spiritual Warfare Network,' author of the book *Possessing the Gates of the Enemy*, and director of Generals of Intercession. She says that "Spiritual mapping … is the investigation of a city to discover any area of penetration that Satan has made, so as to prevent the expansion of the Gospel and the evangelization of that city for Christ." [2]

Dr. C. Peter Wagner says, "Through spiritual mapping we attempt to see the world around us as it really is, and not as it appears to be." [3] The apostle Paul corroborates this by saying; *"…while we do not look at the things which are seen, but at the things which are not seen. For the things which are seen are temporary, but the things which are not seen are eternal"* (2 Corinthians 4:18 italics added).

My friend, Harold Caballeros, founder and pastor of the 'El Shaddai' church in Guatemala City, member of the 'Spiritual Warfare Network,' and regional coordinator in Central America for the 'United Prayer Movement of AD 2000,' defines spiritual mapping as follows:

> "Spiritual mapping is one of the revelations God has given us to reach billions in our generation. It is one of God's secrets that enables us to use our spiritual 'radar' to show us the world's situations from God's perspective, spiritually, and not how we generally see, naturally (physically)… Spiritual mapping fulfills the same role as espionage for the CIA - Central Intelligence Agency - fulfills in times of war. It will indicate what is at the enemy's frontline. It is a spiritual weapon, sophisticated and strategic, powerful in God, and helps us in casting down strongholds."[4]

Victor Lorenzo, who is originally from Argentina, works with 'Harvest Time Evangelism.' His gift of discernment has allowed him to do a spiritual mapping of the cities of Resistencia and La Plata, Argentina. He is the Secretary of the 'Spiritual Warfare Network'(south end) and the National Coordinator for the 'United Prayer Movement for AD 2000.' He gives us the following definition: "Spiritual mapping combines investigation, divine revelation, and confirmed evidence to give the exact information regarding identities, strategies, and methods employed by the power of darkness to influence the people and churches of a certain region. It is like the intelligence service of the army that infiltrates the enemy's frontlines to know their plans and strongholds. As Kyell Sjoberg says: 'Spiritual mapping is like spiritual espionage.'"[5]

If I were to define spiritual mapping, I would say that it is God's revelation of the spiritual condition of the world in which we live. It is a vision that takes us beyond our natural senses and, through the Holy Spirit, reveals to us the hosts of spiritual wickedness that rule over cities and nations.

WE MUST FIND THE LOST TO SAVE THE LOST

Spiritual mapping provides a picture of the situation in heavenly places. Spiritual mapping is to an intercessor what x-rays are to a surgeon. It is a supernatural vision that shows us the frontlines of the enemy, his position, his numbers, his weapons, and overall the strategy to defeat him. Spiritual mapping is a process, not an event. Through investigation and understanding of cultural, historical, political, and religious backgrounds of towns we are able to discern and know the reasons for current situations in a town. Spiritual maps help the 'found' find the 'lost'. They pinpoint where the 'unreached people' groups are, who they are, what their beliefs are, and what their roots in idolatry are.

The spiritual understanding of many Christians, who in spite of all their labor do not see fruit, is the same as the child who called his mother to tell her he was lost. When the mother asked him where he was, he sincerely answered, "If I knew that, I wouldn't be lost." Perhaps this anecdote will help us comprehend the urgency of the need for spiritual mapping, because if we don't know where we're going, any road may lead there.

Let me clarify that not all spiritual mapping will allow us to know the works of darkness. Often we see areas of redemptive work and the various gifts and abilities of cities and nations. No matter how this knowledge is used, it will always be to the benefit of the cities and nations being mapped and for the proclamation of the Gospel.

"All investigations are born out of a vibrant and perfect relationship with God and deep love for the lost.

The results can be verified or discredited easily through history, present observations, and the Word of God." [6]

As we can see, spiritual mapping is a process of studying the roots of towns that reveal the supernatural dimension of that town. As a result, we obtain a detailed spiritual map with borders, capitals, cities, and battlefronts, completely different from what can be seen in the natural or political realm. In the spiritual world map, beliefs such as Buddhism, Hinduism, Islam, Spiritualism, Voodoo, 'Santeria,' 'Macumba,' and materialism are not simply philosophies, but true spiritual strongholds that have billions of human souls enslaved and bound to a powerful hierarchy of demonic authorities. "For we do not wrestle against flesh and blood, but against principalities, against powers, against the rulers of the darkness of this age, against spiritual hosts of wickedness in the heavenly places" (Ephesians 6:12).

THE VALUE OF SPIRITUAL MAPPING

Spiritual mapping is a great source of information for spiritual warfare. The purpose of warfare is to reach the lost and destroy the works of the evil one. Therefore, spiritual mapping is valuable for evangelization and for determining the strategies that should be taken in battle. The more we know about the enemy's methods and strategies, the more effective we will be in counterattacking his assaults, and in destroying his strongholds. The result of knowing these things could produce a spiritual revival in our regions, cities, and nations, as well as political and social reform that will change the conditions of an area and bring spiritual liberty to many.

George Otis, Jr., says, "Those who take the time to talk with God and to listen to Him, before venturing into any ministry, not only will find themselves in the right place, at the right time, but will also know what they should do when they get there." [7]

I was watching a boxing match a few years ago between the famous boxer, Mohamed Ali (Cassius Clay) and another boxer whose name I don't recall. Ali's skill and dexterity allowed him to play with his opponent. To no avail, Ali's competitor chased him around the ring, throwing punches in the air. It was obvious that he did not have the ability or training to win the match with Ali. Many Christians are like this boxer, throwing punches in the air and working too hard. Before long they tire out and faint. In the long run they become victims instead of victors and leave the battlefield frustrated, disappointed, and depressed. We are reminded of the biblical verdict, *"My people are destroyed for lack of knowledge"* (Hosea 4:6 italics added).

Spiritual mapping helps the 'found' find the 'lost'

For many Christians, prayer and intercession to reach their communities and cities for Christ is no more than a habitual expression to God demonstrating their good intentions. Though they recognize the authority and lordship of Jesus Christ, they possess neither the passion to reach the lost nor the boldness to make an impact in the spiritual realm. They are like many mealtime prayers: a habit or ritual, but not a sincere appreciation for divine provision.

Before attempting to attack and re-conquer our cities and nations for Christ, it is necessary to understand the circumstances and the nature of the conflict so that we are able to bind the strong man and set the captives free in Jesus' name.

> "But Jesus knew their thoughts, and said to them: 'Every kingdom divided against itself is brought to desolation, and every city or house divided against itself will not stand. If Satan casts out Satan, he is divided against himself. How then will his kingdom stand? And if I cast out demons by Beelzebub, by whom do your sons cast them out? Therefore they shall be your judges. But if I cast out demons by the Spirit of God, surely the Kingdom of God has come upon you. Or how can one enter a strong man's house and plunder his goods, unless he first binds the strong man? And then he will plunder his house.'"
> (Matthew 12:25-29)

The key is in knowing Satan's schemes and plots so he will not have the advantage over us. God wants to reveal His multifaceted wisdom to the Church. This wisdom is acquired through a careful study of God's Word, much time in intimate communion with God, and a thorough understanding of the cultural, religious, economic, and social roots of towns, villages, etc.

When king David formed his army, many who came to him already knew what needed to be done. "...of the sons of Issachar who had understanding of the times, to know what Israel ought to do, their chiefs were two hundred; and all their brethren were at their command" (Chronicles 12:32).

To discern and know what to do, we need to have three types of information: historical, social, and spiritual. This is precisely what is acquired through spiritual mapping. Once we have this information, we can develop a battle plan to retake our cities and nations for Christ.

Notes

[1] Otis, Jr., p. 85.

[2] C. Peter Wagner, *Breaking Strongholds in your City*. Ventura CA: Regal Books, 1993. p. 277.

[3] Ibid., p.4.

[4] Ibid., p. 125.

[5] Ibid., pp. 177-178.

[6] Ibid., p.33.

[7] George Otis, Jr., *Operation Second Chance*. A document previously distributed by the Sentinel Group, 1992, p. 19.

———————◆———————

CHAPTER TWELVE

BIBLICAL BACKGROUND

And the Lord spoke to Moses saying, 'Send men to spy out the land of Canaan, which I am giving to the children of Israel; from each tribe of their fathers you shall send a man, every one a leader among them' (Numbers 13:1-2).

In my travels through Latin America and Southeast Asia, I've realized that when the term 'spiritual mapping' is used, many are perplexed because it is not used, as such, in the Bible. Yet, when it is defined, it can be easily seen in many passages of the Old and New Testaments. Often the Bible speaks of the conflicts of cosmic forces, of the reality of the spiritual realm, of the importance of spiritual warfare, of the necessity to identify the enemy's camp, and of the existence of celestial and demonic beings and their influence in our lives and destiny.

The Church in the western world is highly responsible for the indifference towards spiritual matters; philosophies, humanistic sciences, and materialism have infiltrated seminaries and pulpits. Nevertheless, every human being has the Creator's indelible imprint in his being and has a sense of the supernatural. This is why an individual will seek out other forms of spiritual satisfaction when he does not find the answers to his questions in the Church. This explains the reason for the growth of eastern religions and philosophies, Satanism, witchcraft, spiritism, new age philosophy, etc. in our society.

Though it hasn't been officially voiced (and it will not be because there is no official representative), the evangelical fundamental church demonstrates an indifference towards the theology of spiritual warfare. It is a lack of knowledge or understanding in this area that goes back centuries. But God is now releasing this knowledge and understanding to equip and prepare an army for the end time spiritual conflicts; a simple religious congregation will not get the job done.

My purpose in this section is to provide some scripture references that enable us to find a biblical background for spiritual mapping.

PREPARING TO CONQUER CANAAN

All we need is a little discernment to perceive that some scripture passages make mention of spiritual mapping. For example, in Numbers 13:17-21, we find the following:

> "Then Moses sent them to spy out the land of Canaan, and said to them, 'Go up this way into the South, and go up to the mountains, and see what the land is like: Whether the people who dwell in it are strong or weak, few or many; whether the land they dwell in is good or bad; whether the cities they inhabit are like camps or strongholds; whether the land is rich or poor; and whether there are forests there or not. Be of good courage. And bring some of the fruit of the land.' Now the

time was the season of the first ripe grapes. So they went up and spied out the land from the Wilderness of Zin as far as Rehob, near the entrance of Hamath."

Moses was a powerful man in Egypt. Due to divine providence, he was a Prince. "But when he was set out, Pharaoh's daughter took him away and brought him up as her own son" (Acts 7:21).

According to the historian Flavius Josephus in his book *Antiquities of the Jews,* Moses was trained for battle in Egypt and was the general who led the Egyptian armies in the conquest of Ethiopia.[1] In addition, he was a man mighty in words and deeds. To prepare the people of Israel for the conquest of Canaan, Moses sent spies to the South land with special instructions to observe it's topographic conditions (natural and physical conditions, size of the city, the size of it's army, etc.). The expedition lasted 40 days. Afterwards a detailed report of their findings was presented.

"And they returned from spying out the land after forty days. Now they departed and came back to Moses and Aaron and all the congregation of the children of Israel in the Wilderness of Paran, at Kadesh; they brought back word to them and to all the congregation, and showed them the fruit of the land. Then they told him, and said: 'We went to the land where you sent us. It truly flows with milk and honey, and this is its fruit. Nevertheless, the people who dwell in the land are strong; the cities are fortified and very large; moreover we saw the descendants of Anak there. The Amalekites dwell in the land of the South; the Hittites, the Jebusites, and the Amorites dwell in the mountains; and the Canaanites dwell by the sea along the banks of the Jordan.' Then Caleb quieted the people before Moses, and said, 'Let us go up at once and take possession, for we are well able to overcome it.' But the men who had gone up with him said, 'We are not able to go up against the people, for they are stronger than we.' And they gave the children of Israel a bad report of the land, which they had spied out, saying, 'The land through which we have gone as spies is a land that devours its inhabitants, and all the people whom we saw in it are men of great stature. There we saw the giants (the descendant of Anak came from the giants); and we were like grasshoppers in our own sight, and so we were in their sight.'" (Numbers 13:25-33)

In this passage, we see an example of investigation before action in the spiritual realm. This shows us the necessity of spiritual mapping in order to know the strengths and weaknesses of our adversary.

JOSHUA AND SPIRITUAL MAPPING

Another example of espionage can be found in the book of Joshua.

"Then Joshua said to the children of Israel: 'How long will you neglect to go and possess the land which the Lord God of your fathers has given you? Pick out from among you three men from each tribe, and I will send them; they shall rise and go through the land, survey it according to their inheritance, and come back to me. And they shall divide it into seven parts, Judah shall remain in their territory on the South, and the house of Joseph shall remain in their territory on the north. You shall therefore survey the land in seven

parts and bring the survey here to me, that I may cast
lots for you here before the Lord our God.'"
(Joshua 18:3-6)

This veteran of the Canaan expedition now sends 21 men
to survey the land and return with a complete, mapped out
description of the territory. Consequently, Joshua was able to
divide the land based on the results of the investigation and
the map describing the region. Those who "drew" the maps
were called "cartographers" or "mappers." Without a doubt,
the spiritual application of this passage gives us the basis to
'possess the land' once we've retaken it from the enemy's
power. Surely, after the investigation, Joshua divides the land;
however, I would like to draw your attention to the necessity
of planning and mapping territories before taking any action.
Although in both the Numbers and Joshua passages, the Bible
is not clear on the spiritual implication of mapping, it is evident that the conquest of these regions brought about cultural,
social, and spiritual changes.

EZEKIEL DESIGNS A MAP OF JERUSALEM

In the book of Ezekiel, we find a wonderful example of the
spiritual implication of a map of Jerusalem. God instructs the
prophet to begin a spiritual battle in prayer and to lay siege
against the city to cast out the iniquity of Israel and Judah.

"You also, son of man, take a clay tablet and lay it
before you, and portray on it a city, Jerusalem. Lay
siege against it, build a siege wall against it, and heap
up a mound against it; set camps against it also, and
place battering rams against it all around. Moreover
take for yourself an iron plate, and set it as an iron wall
between you and the city. Set your face against it, and

it shall be besieged, and you shall lay siege against it.
This will be a sign to the house of Israel. Lie also on
your left side, and lay the iniquity of the house of Israel upon it. According to the number of the days that
you lie on it, you shall bear their iniquity. For I have
laid on you the years of their iniquity, according to the
number of the days, three hundred and ninety days; so
you shall bear, the iniquity of the house of Israel. And
when you have completed them, lie again on your right
side; then you shall bear the iniquity of the house of
Judah forty days. I have laid on you a day for each
year. Therefore you shall set your face toward the siege
of Jerusalem; your arm shall be uncovered and you
shall prophesy against it. And surely I will restrain
you so that you cannot turn from one side to another
till you have ended the days of your siege."
(Ezekiel 4:1-8)

The judgment God decreed for the city of Jerusalem was
the result of the spiritual condition of its inhabitants.

"Thus says the Lord God: 'This is Jerusalem; I have
set her in the midst of the nations and the countries all
around her. She has rebelled against My judgements
by doing wickedness more than the nations, and against
My statutes more than the countries that are all around
her; for they have refused My judgements, and they
have not walked in My statues. Therefore thus says
the Lord God: Because you have multiplied disobedience more than the nations that are all around you,
have not walked in My statutes nor kept My judgments,
nor even done according to the judgments of the nations that are all around you. Therefore, thus says the

Lord God: Indeed I, even I, am against you and will execute judgments in your midst in the sight of the nations. And I will do among you what I have never done, and the like of which I will never do again, because of all your abominations. Therefore fathers shall eat their sons in your midst, and sons shall eat their fathers; and I will execute judgement among you, and all of you who remain I will scatter to all the winds. Therefore, as I live, says the Lord God, surely, because you have defiled My sanctuary with all your detestable things and with all your abomination, therefore I will also diminish you; My eye will not spare, nor will I have any pity. One-third of you shall die of the pestilence, and be consumed with famine in your midst; and one-third shall fall by the sword all around you; and I will scatter another third to all the winds, and I will draw out a sword after them. Thus shall My anger be spent, and I will cause My fury to rest upon them, and I will be avenged; and they shall know that I, the Lord, have spoken it in My zeal, when I have spent My fury upon them.'" (Ezekiel 5:5-13)

In conclusion, spiritual mapping allows us to discern and prepare strategies for spiritual warfare. We must enter into it through prayer and fasting to weaken the enemy's strongholds and open spiritual doors for evangelism. According to George Otis, Jr., spiritual mapping must answer these questions:
1. What problems are occurring?
2. What are the reasons for these problems?
3. What can we do to change the situation?

SPIRITUAL MAPPING AND THE TAKING OF A CITY

In the book of Acts, we find a clear passage on the importance of spiritual mapping and its relevancy to seizing a city given over to idolatry and human philosophies. While Paul was in Athens waiting for his friends, Timothy and Silas, he was able to thoroughly observe the city. He visited the market places, conversed with philosophers and studied their writings. With a burden in his heart, he presented himself "in the midst of the Areopagus" and said:

> "Men of Athens, I perceive that in all things you are very religious; for as I was passing through and considering the objects of your worship, I even found an altar with this inscription: 'To the Unknown God.' Therefore, the One whom you worship without knowing, Him I proclaim to you." (Acts 17:22-23)

Because of his observations, Paul was able to appeal to the people, evangelizing them and leading them to repentance. He said:

> "Truly, these times of ignorance God overlooked, but now commands all men everywhere to repent, because He has appointed a day on which He will judge the world in righteousness by the Man whom He has ordained. He has given assurance of this to all by raising Him from the dead." (Acts 17:30-31)

Notes
[1] Paul L. Maier, *Josephus: The Essential Writings*. Grand Rapids, MI: Kregel Publications, 1988, p. 47.

CHAPTER THIRTEEN

———————◆———————

THE SPIRIT OF DESTRUCTION

The thief comes to kill, steal, and destroy. The word destroy in Greek is *Apollyon,* which means, 'destroyer.' "And they had as king over them the angel of the bottomless pit, whose name in Hebrew is Abaddon, but in Greek he has the name Apollyon." (Revelations 9:11)

"'Most assuredly, I say to you, he who does not enter the sheepfold by the door, but climbs up some other way, the same is a thief and a robber. But he who enters by the door is the shepherd of the sheep. To him the doorkeeper opens, and the sheep hear his voice; and he calls his own sheep by name and leads them out. And when he brings out his own sheep, he goes before them; and the sheep follow him, for they know his voice. Yet, they will by no means follow a stranger, but will flee from him, for they do not know the voice of strangers.' Jesus used this illustration, but they did

not understand the things which He spoke to them."
(John 10:1-6)

The apostle Paul indicates that due to Israel's lust for evil it sinned against God and fell victim to the destroyer.

"Moreover, brethren, I do not want you to be unaware that all our fathers were under the cloud, all passed through the sea, all were baptized into Moses in the cloud and in the sea, all ate the same spiritual food, and all drank the same spiritual drink. For they drank of that spiritual Rock that followed them, and that Rock was Christ. But with most of them God was not well pleased, for their bodies were scattered in the wilderness. Now these things became our examples, to the intent that we should not lust after evil things as they also lusted. And do not become idolaters as were some of them. As it is written, 'The people sat down to eat and drink, and rose up to play.' Nor let us commit sexual immorality, as some of them did, and in one day twenty three thousand fell; nor let us tempt Christ, as some of them also tempted, and were destroyed by serpents; nor complain, as some of them also complained, and were destroyed by the destroyer."
(1 Corinthians 10:1-10)

The term for destroyer in Hebrew is Abaddon. The violent one, the destroyer, *Apollyon* or *Abaddon,* is known mainly as the spirit of violence.

"But Job answered and said: How have you helped him who is without power? How have you saved the arm that has no strength? How have you counseled one who has no wisdom? And how have you declared sound advice to many? To whom have you uttered words? And whose spirit came from you? The dead tremble, those under the waters and those inhabiting them. Sheol is naked before Him, and Destruction has no covering." (Job 26:1-6)

"Concerning the works of men, by the word of Your lips, I have kept away from the paths of the destroyer." (Psalm 17:4)

COLOMBIA, SOUTH AMERICA: A CLASSIC STUDY ON THE SPIRIT OF VIOLENCE.

Colombia's inheritance has been violence. It was founded and established in violence. Colombia is known as one of the most violent nations of the entire world, particularly the city of Medellin. The only other city with the same kind of reputation is Colombo, Sri Lanka, where the war between Hindus, Moslems, and Buddhists is destroying the nation.

Medellin was established in 1616 by a Marshall named Robledo. The Spanish "conquistadors" founded the city through violence and greed. They got rid of the indigenous people and liquidated anyone that interfered with them and their search for gold. People from Basque, Spain, and certain Jewish people immigrated to the region in search of gold, and just as in the wild, wild west of the United States, these people were self-reliant and resolved all their conflicts through violence, killing one another because of politics, religion, or honor. One of the regions most opposed to the gospel was Antioquia, particularly its capital which is referred to as the Rome of Latin America.

In cities such as Union, Santa Rosa de Osos, Medellin,

Entreros, San Pedro, Segovia, etc., there were brave soldiers of God's Army. North American missionaries and their Colombian disciples such as Benigno Mantilla, Jose Gutierrez, Jesus Zuleta, Carmen Husma, Julio Orozco, Henry Parra, and many more suffered persecution and shed their blood for the gospel of Jesus Christ. Segovia, so called in memory of Segovia, Spain, manifested its violent spirit to prove faithfulness to the region, as did their Spaniard forefathers, in the infamous 'faith acts' which were carried out by the burning alive of all "heretics." Territorial spirits of violence and greed still prevail in the country, and particularly in this region. "And from the days of John the Baptist until now the kingdom of heaven suffers violence and the violent take it by force" (Matthew 11:12).

"Most assuredly, I say to you, unless a grain of wheat falls into the ground and dies, it remains alone; but if it dies, it produces much grain." (John 12.24 italics added) The blood of many of these martyrs has been the 'seed' that is now undergoing an explosive revival in the country. Colombia has to prepare itself, for it is the hour of God's visitation. Spiritual warfare is most intense during the time of God's visitation; it was so during Jesus' time, it is so today. Just as with the wave of political and religious violence that gripped the country in the year 1948 and thereafter, called the 'Bogotanazo' (due to the assassination of Jorge Eliecer Gaitan), there came a great spiritual revival.

In 1943, the evangelical church in Colombia numbered approximately 3,000. By 1960 it had grown to 30,654 baptized members and it doubled to 63,810 in 1960. By 1970, the 'Protestant' community had grown to 255,240 evangelicals. Today there are approximately one million evangelicals (information provided by B.H. Pearson in *My God Just Passed By*, published in 1972 by the 'Mision Interamericana,' founded in Colombia in 1943).

Gonzalo Jimenez De Quesada conquered Bogota, the 'gray' city and capital of the 'Chibcha' empire, in 1536. Jimenez renamed it 'Santa Fe de Bogota.' Though this city was also founded with violence and destruction, it has experienced a great and explosive revival! This revival was brought on, in part, by the unity of Pastors and by God's people working as a team. There was no star player, but instead a team with intercessors and frontline warriors working together to obtain the victory over the adversary.

◆

PERSECUTION DID NOT DESTROY THE CHURCH; IT SERVED TO STRENGTHEN IT

◆

On Monday, December 16, 1968, 'El Tiempo,' Colombia's most important newspaper, printed the following news: **Evangelicals Make Known the Religious Freedom That Exists in the Nation**. The article begins by saying "30,000 evangelicals marched yesterday through downtown Bogota."

Persecution did not destroy the Church; it served to strengthen it. The Body of Christ grows through crisis. Historically, revival has been the result of violent persecution against the Church of Jesus Christ. The challenge to those who hold the keys to the spiritual gates of the cities is to seize these cities and nations for Christ. How is this accomplished? The battle may be initiated by following these steps:

1. Raise up an army of prayer warriors, intercessors who will fast and bind the strong man, the prince of the powers of the air assigned to our countries and cities.

2. Discern the Territorial Spirits assigned to each area and war against them with opposite spirits, for example:
   a.   If it's violence, counterattack with peace.
   b.   If it's hate, counterattack with love.
   c.   If it's greed, counterattack with generosity.
3.   Prepare the people: mobilize God's army. Equip the people with spiritual weapons and with the knowledge and wisdom of God to recognize the enemy's tactics so they may oppose the enemy and come out of the battle victoriously.

WE MUST HAVE A PREPARED ARMY

Every army suffers losses and casualties in battle, yet the more prepared the army is, the more unified the commanders and generals are, and the quicker and more efficient the battle is, the fewer the casualties (the United States Army in the Persian Gulf was a wonderful example of this). Destruction, cost, and fatalities are greatest when there is confusion, lack of communication, independent attitudes, etc.

The *gatekeepers* have to prepare the spiritual soil of their cities and nations. At the precise hour, and in God's timing, they should lead a surprise attack using all their weapons. This will bring to your community the greatest revival it has ever experienced.

What will happen to the Christian church in America? We have the challenge of becoming a vital force of major importance in this continent. As millions are won for Christ, nations will experience a sense of stability, balance, purpose, and peace, teaching and demonstrating values of love, peace, faith, sacrifice, discipline, responsibility, and giving dignity to every human being. When all these things come together, the Church will enjoy fellowship with God.

PART FIVE

THE WEAPONS
OF OUR WARFARE

"For the weapons of our warfare are not carnal but mighty in God for pulling down strongholds."

(2 Corinthians 10:4)

———————◆———————

CHAPTER FOURTEEN

THE WEAPONS OF OUR WARFARE

Every Christian is called to be a soldier in God's army. Jehovah is called the Lord of hosts. Jehovah Tsebath is the title of the commanding general of the armies. It is He who promises to give us the victory and make us more than conquerors. He stood with David and gave him the victory over the Philistines, the Moabites, and the Arameans. It was the Lord of hosts who defended Jerusalem from the hand of the Assyrian king for the love of David His servant and for the love of His name. *"When a strong man, fully armed, guards his own palace, his goods are in peace"* (Luke 11:21 italics added).

> "For out of Jerusalem shall go a remnant, and those who escape from Mount Zion. The zeal of the Lord of hosts will do this, Therefore, thus says the Lord concerning the king of Assyria: 'He shall not come into this city, nor shoot an arrow there, nor come before it

with shield, nor build a siege mound against it. By the way that he came, by the same shall he return; and he shall not come into this city,' says the Lord. 'For I will defend this city, to save for My own sake and for My servant David's sake.'" (2 Kings 19:31-34)

It is the Lord of hosts who promises never to leave us or forsake us. He who is the Captain and Author of our salvation promises to descend from His throne to fight in defense of His people. "Like birds flying about, so will the Lord of hosts defend Jerusalem. Defending, He will also deliver it; passing over, He will preserve it." (Isaiah 31:5)

The Christian is a citizen of the Kingdom of the Living God, our spiritual Jerusalem that holds the assembly of the children of heaven, whose names have been written in the Lamb's book of life from the foundation of the world.

THE LORD AS OUR BANNER

Another name for the Lord is Jehovah-Nissi, which means "Jehovah is my banner." The banner or flag represents the nation and the triumphant army. Moses used this name to declare that God would always defeat the enemy as long as the Israelite people followed him. We see how the Amalekites fought against Israel at Rephidim. As long as the people of God were engaged in battle and Moses kept the rod of the Lord raised, the Israelites were victorious. But when Moses grew tired and brought his arms down, the Amalekites prevailed. However, when Aaron and Hur began helping Moses hold his arms up, Joshua was able to lead the army into victory; totally destroying the enemy with the sword. To commemorate this victory: "…Moses built an altar and called its name, 'The Lord is my Banner,' for he said, 'Because the

Lord has sworn: the Lord will have war with Amalek from generation to generation'" (Exodus 17:15-16).

Spiritual warfare deals with conflict in the spiritual realm. "Our battle is not against flesh and blood," (human beings). For this reason God has given us spiritual weapons to fight battles, for though we walk (live) in the flesh, we do not war (battle) according to the flesh. For the weapons of our warfare are not carnal (human), but mighty in God for pulling down strongholds.

> "For though we walk in the flesh, we do not war according to the flesh. For the weapons of our warfare are not carnal but mighty in God for pulling down strongholds, casting down arguments and every high thing that exalts itself against the knowledge of God, bringing every thought into captivity to the obedience of Christ." (2 Corinthians 10:3-5)

To protect our possessions, God has given us the following weapons, so that being equipped and well trained in them, victory will be insured.

- Prayer and fasting
- The blood of Jesus
- The name of Jesus
- The Holy Spirit
- The Word of God
- Praise and worship
- The ministry of angels
- The love of God

The book of Ephesians is the instruction manual for the army of God. Paul concludes the revelation given to him by the Holy Spirit by challenging the believer to be fully clothed with the armor of God so that the armies of God "will be able

to withstand in the evil day, and having done all, to stand"
(Ephesians 6:13).

"Finally, my brethren, be strong in the Lord and the power of
His might" (Ephesians 6:10). The term 'be strong' is the Greek
for 'energeo.' This verse can be interpreted as: Be filled with
power in the Lord and in the power (kratos) of His might
(ischus). These three terms are the training instructions on
the use of the armor and weapons given to us.

Energeo: Energy or power with evidence. It refers to the use
and application of power.

Kratos: Vigor; it also means exploits, which is to say the
result of using the power.

Ischus: Strength signifies power and authority received
through inheritance. An inherent strength that allows us to
resist.

> "...the eyes of your understanding being enlightened;
> that you may know what is the hope of His calling,
> what are the riches of the glory of His inheritance in
> the saints, and what is the exceeding greatness of His
> power toward us who believe, according to the work-
> ing of His mighty power."   (Ephesians 1:18-19)

VICTORY WILL COME TO
THE BODY OF CHRIST WHEN WE
ARE UNIFIED IN THE SPIRIT

Once we understand our authority, our calling, and our
weapons, we are ordered to submit to the Captain of the heavenly armies, to resist the devil, which is to say, to stand in
opposition as an antihistamine. "Put on the whole armor of

God, that you may be able to stand against the wiles of the devil" (Ephesians 6:11).

The command is to put on the whole armor of God so that we may be able to stand firm, maintaining our ground without stumbling or backing down from the enemy's schemes (methodeia), lies, tricks, deception, or any method of attack from the 'father of lies.' "Therefore take up the **whole armor** of God, that you may be able to withstand in the evil day, and having done all, to stand" (Ephesians 6:13 emphasis added). We all must put on the whole armor of God so that we may stand.

"Stand therefore, having girded your waist with truth, having put on the breastplate of righteousness, and having shod your feet with the preparation of the gospel of peace; above all, taking the shield of faith with which you will be able to quench all the fiery darts of the wicked one. And take the helmet of salvation, and the sword of the Spirit, which is the Word of God." (Ephesians 6:14-17)

How We Use Our Armor

The breastplate of righteousness is understanding our position in Christ; that is to say, we are justified in Christ through His blood. We walk using our feet (Ephesians 4:1&5:1). Our walking should always be with the gospel of peace. In addition, take the shield of faith by which you will be able to quench all the fiery darts of the wicked one, the helmet of salvation, and the sword of the Spirit, which is the Word of God. "But let us who are of the day be sober, putting on the breastplate of faith and love, and as a helmet the hope of salvation" (1Thessalonians 5:8).

The helmet is the protective head covering which protects the mind, will, and emotions. The sword (machaira) is an offensive weapon more clearly described by the word Machete. In the Middle East there are various types of swords: Long swords, sharp pointed swords, and sharp edged swords. But the swords used by the Roman soldiers were short, pointed, and double-edged. This sword was designed to destroy, to confine, and to resist the enemy's attack till the enemy was conquered (Nikao). Christ disarmed the enemy and has given us the necessary weapons to overcome this enemy. In Christ Jesus we are more than conquerors. This means that as the Church, victory will come to the Body of Christ when we are unified in the Spirit. God has given us a double-edged sword to destroy all of the enemy's attacks.

"How could one chase a thousand, and two put ten thousand to flight, unless their Rock had sold them, and the Lord had surrendered them?" (Deuteronomy 32:30) The call is for the **whole** Body of Christ to be united in battle, not just certain individuals. Spiritual warfare is effective when it is carried out in the fullness of the Body of Christ.

In marriage we are to be both physically and mentally faithful. In our individual life, we are to walk in integrity. And in our Christian walk, we are not to compromise our spiritual, emotional, physical, or financial principals.

"You will chase your enemies, and they shall fall by the sword before you. Five of you shall chase a hundred, and a hundred of you shall put ten thousand to flight; your enemies shall fall by the sword before you."
(Leviticus 26:7-8 italics added)

CHAPTER FIFTEEN

PRAYER OPENS DOORS
FOR THE GOSPEL

Continue earnestly in prayer, be vigilant in it with thanks-giving; meanwhile praying also for us, that God would open to us a door for the Word, to speak the mystery of Christ, for which I am also in chains, that I may make it manifest, as I ought to speak (Colossians 4:2-4).

A major part of the information contained in this chapter has been obtained from a conference on intercession. My friend John D. Robb presented this material at a conference to The International Society for Frontier Missions in September 1990. The conference's title was "Prayer, A Strategic Weapon for Frontier Missions." The information from this conference was then shared with the members of 'The Spiritual Warfare Network' at its second conference that was held November 1990. There were some changes in the facts given at the original conference, due to the miraculous fall of the Soviet Government. However, the general content of the conference was relevant, contemporary, and impacts greatly the importance of intercession in spiritual warfare.

The apostle Paul urged the Christians of his generation to, *"Continue earnestly in prayer, being vigilant in it with thanksgiving"*(Colossians 4:2 italics added).

HOW PRAYER CHANGED GUINEA, WEST AFRICA

Don McCurry's International Ministry to the Moslems is an illustration of being earnest and vigilant in prayer. A number of years ago, Don McCurry visited Guinea, West Africa. He found that a Marxist leader named Sekou Toure had ousted all but two missionaries and was torturing all political prisoners. After observing this, McCurry and twelve national pastors began to intercede for the country and the two missionaries. Their first point of intercession was for the overthrow of this tyrannical Marxist leader who had closed the doors to any future missionary efforts.

Secondly, maps of the country were placed in their prayer and meeting rooms. Together in prayer, they placed their hands over specific regions that had not been reached with the Gospel of Jesus Christ. They prayed prophetically and agreed for an advancement and establishment of Christian ministries from among themselves. Less than a year later, Sekou Toure was rendered powerless. A benevolent leader replaced Sekou Toure and once again the doors to missionaries were opened. Today, each one of those prayer partners occupies a national level position regarding missionary endeavors.

When Jonathan Goforth planned to start a new work in Honan, a province in China, Hudson Taylor wrote him these words: "Brother, if you want to win that Province, you must go on your knees." His advice still stands strong today.

In recent years, we have seen God destroy anti-Christian

strongholds in the Soviet Union, Romania, and Albania. When God's people begin to focus their prayers on other spiritually difficult places such as Mauritania, Morocco, Libya, Turkey, or Saudi Arabia, we can expect God to intervene and do the same.

BREAKING THE CONTROL

Spiritual warfare breaks the control that the powers of darkness have over towns, cities, and nations. The enemy's chains have to be broken in order for frontier missions to progress. Spiritual darkness and chains of servitude often bind those who haven't been reached with the Truth. These chains bind cities and countries with principalities and powers that seek to control the affairs of the occupants.

Presently, in the world of missions, we are experiencing a rediscovery of spiritual power that results in reaching the lost in much the same way Yahweh confronted the gods of Egypt and the Baals of Mount Carmel. The thrust is the same, a powerful spiritual encounter between the true God and false deities, those spiritual beings who control segments of human events.

Dr. C. Peter Wagner, in a symposium on evangelistic power at Fuller Theological Seminary, affirms the following: "Satan delegates to high ranking members of the hierarchy of evil spirits the control of nations, regions, tribes, towns, neighborhoods, and other significant human effort. His main objective is to hinder God from being exalted. This is accomplished by the action of lower ranking demons."

Ephesians 6 indicates that all Christians are involved in an invisible battle with the powers of darkness. This invisible battle is intensified with those missionaries, intercessors, and pastors who are involved in frontier missions. The apostle

Paul says that our battle or literal 'fight' has to be shaped by a spirit led prayer. In this cosmic battle, we have two offensive weapons at our disposal: the sword of the spirit, which is the Word of God, and prayer. With this in mind, if we are to accomplish missionary outreach in towns, cities, and countries, we have to learn to use prayer as an offensive weapon to evict the powers of darkness. Dr. Wagner makes this implication: "If the hypothesis concerning territorial spirits is correct and if we can learn how to break their strongholds through the power of God, then the resistance/receptivity axis could change overnight."

Francis Frangipane points out similar traits when he writes about the strongholds that the powers of darkness have over people groups: "There are Satanic strongholds over cities and communities; there are strongholds that have influence in churches and individuals. These strongholds exist in the thought patterns and ideas that govern an individual ... communities and nations. Before shouting the victory, these strongholds have to be demolished and Satan's weapons destroyed. Then the powerful weapons of the Word and the Spirit will effectively plunder Satan's dwelling."

Studies of pagan belief systems prove the reality of what is depicted in Ephesians 6, the book of Daniel, and other scripture passages.

- The **Burmese** believe in supernatural beings called NATS. These are assigned in hierarchical order and have control over natural phenomena, villages, regions, and nations.
- In **Thailand**, there are village and regional spirits. The village spirits are subordinate to regional spirits. Often, in villages, a pillar or dwelling place for guardian spirits is built. A Christian Missionary Alliance missionary tells of what she and a co-worker discovered:

"Once this pillar was erected, we could sense an increase in oppression and lack of spiritual receptivity." Also, an OMF missionary has identified national principalities that govern over all of Thailand.

♦ In **India**, we find a similar belief system of guardian spirits in villages and other regions. Frequently these spirits are associated with sicknesses, sudden deaths, and catastrophes. Kali, the goddess of destruction, is a regional deity known particularly among the inhabitants of West Bengal, Calcutta. Anyone who visits Calcutta can see the devastation that the worship of Kali has brought to the city and its people. Christian workers who live in Calcutta describe the severe oppression and serious division among the churches. Strangely enough, the Christian churches have never united to pray for the city nor have they taken the offensive against the powers of darkness.

♦ A book written about the country of **Zimbabwe**, Africa, reveals how each region, city, and village is bound to fall under the control of territorial spirits. A leader of the Assemblies of God in Nigeria, who was a high ranking official in the occult before his conversion, states that Satan had assigned twelve spirits to his control, and each of these spirits had control over 600 demons. He also testifies to the following: "I was in contact with all of the spirits that controlled each village in Nigeria and in each major city, where there was a temple."

♦ In a recent meeting with a well-known **Japanese** evangelist and Japanese missionaries, I was surprised to discover how the Japanese are still bound by occult practices. We can be fooled by the sophistication of Japanese technology and never notice that a high percentage of Japanese still visit their Shinto temples. In addition, their school-aged children still carry amulets, and the Shinto priests are still allowed to dedicate every new building.

♦ The **Western world** is not exempt from pagan belief systems. It is, however, confronting a new phenomenon in the New Age movement. New Age cults call on 'mediums' to make contact with spiritual beings, reestablishing the hold that the powers of darkness originally had, but that had been broken through Christianity and the evangelization of western societies.

PRAYER: A STRATEGIC WEAPON

The problem is that we do not understand that we are in a war without physical boundaries. Hence, we do not see prayer as a strategic weapon. John Piper, a pastor in Minneapolis, puts it this way: "The problem is that many Christians do not believe in spiritual warfare, nor that our invisible enemy is powerful. How then can we make them pray? They say they believe in these truths, but a close look at their life proves differently. There is negligence in the church regarding spiritual things. Bombs are not falling, bullets aren't skimming our heads, there aren't land mines to watch out for, no battle sounds in the horizon; all is well in America, the 'Disneyland' of the universe; so why pray?"

In Mark 3:27, Jesus said something that is especially relevant to frontier missions activity: *"No one can enter a strong man's house and plunder his goods, unless he first binds the strong man. And then he will plunder his house."* (italics added) This affirms the reason why we as Christians cannot impulsively enter and plunder what has belonged to Satan for centuries (portions of humanity under his domain) without first binding those territorial spirits who have control over specific regions. Prayer in the Spirit, based on discovered facts, is a powerful force to bind the strong man in any city, town, or country. In his book, John Dawson shows how one can discover through investigation the links that communities may have with the powers of darkness and how prayer in the unity of the Spirit can break these links.

In Matthew 18:18-19, Jesus gives assurance to those who pray in this manner: "Assuredly, I say to you, whatever you bind on earth will be bound in heaven, and whatever you loose on earth will be loosed in heaven. Again I say to you that if two of you agree on earth concerning anything that they ask, it will be done for them by My Father in heaven."

Spiritual warfare begins when we begin to pray in unity with others. This teaching demonstrates the importance of prayer groups networking to agree in prayer for cities and countries. It seems to me that this will bring the advance.

PRAYER IN THE SPIRIT, BASED ON
DISCOVERED FACTS, IS A POWERFUL FORCE
TO BIND THE STRONG MAN IN ANY CITY,
TOWN, OR COUNTRY

The Greek word for 'bind' in these verses means to 'imprison' or 'chain-up.' God's people praying in unity will limit and imprison the activity of hostile spiritual beings, bringing glory to God's name and expanding His Kingdom on earth. The apostle Paul expresses it this way: "For though we walk in the flesh, we do not war according to the flesh. For the weapons of our warfare are not carnal but mighty in God for pulling down strongholds...." (2 Corinthians 10:3-4).

BINDING THE STRONG MAN THROUGH PRAYER

The experience of Evangelist Omar Cabrera in Argentina high-
lights the power of praying in the Spirit as a weapon against
the occult. Through the years, Cabrera has made a habit of
fasting and praying various days before an evangelistic service in a city he's trying to reach with the gospel. Often spirits
come against him, appearing as grotesque figures, attempting
to hinder his presence in that city and his plans for evangelization. Often they'll say, "You do not have a right to be here,
this is my territory." To which he answers, "On the contrary,
you don't have a right to be here. I bind you by the authority
of Jesus Christ who has all the authority in heaven and on
earth." Immediately the spirit leaves and frequently a higher
principality is sent against Cabrera. In the same manner,
through prayer, Cabrera breaks the yoke of the principality,
which often is a spirit of witchcraft. When the strong man is
bound, the mood of the whole city changes. Frequently, resistance to the gospel is replaced with receptivity and hundreds
of thousands come to Christ with many signs and wonders
taking place. By binding the strong man, Cabrera's congregation has grown from about twenty to being one of the largest
congregations in the world, numbering over 140,000 members.

Though Cabrera's experience may seem strange to us, we
would do well to apply what other Christians are learning in
frontier missions regarding battles won in prayer. During my
travels, the subject of spiritual warfare always comes up when
I'm conducting seminars on missionary strategies to Christians. I'm convinced that unless we identify and bind the strong
man in places we want to reach with the gospel, our strategies
and efforts will amount to nothing. We will not receive an
answer to our prayers unless we bind the strong man.

Could it be that unreached people groups have been unreached due to the force of resisting spirits? Arthur Matthews writes regarding his burden to intercede for two specific areas in Southeast Asia where missionaries have been unsuccessful in penetrating the region with the Gospel. "Therefore, affirming my position with Christ in heavenly places, with the foundation of the Word of God, I put on the whole armor of God so as to resist the devil's lies and his opposition to the gospel." Matthews persisted in prayer until the spiritual condition in those two areas began to change. "The resisting force in the two areas was weakened, making a victory for the Lord possible."

Loren Cunningham, General Director of Youth with a Mission, describes the experience of a three-day prayer and fast he and twelve co-laborers did in 1973. As they prayed, the Lord revealed to them that they should ask for the 'fall' of the 'prince of Greece.' During the same time, YWAM groups in New Zealand and Europe received a similar Word from God. They all obeyed and came against the 'prince of Greece' stronghold. In a twenty-four hour period, a political change took place bringing great freedom to missionary endeavors in the country." [1]

Recently, while brother John Robb was in Senegal conducting a seminar, a leader of the Assemblies of God told him that his denomination began to pray and fast for Moslem outreach. He now sees the people receptive to the gospel and new churches are being established.

PRAYER OPENS DOORS IN PHILIPPINES

In June of 1988, Pastor Marben Lagmay of Santa Maria in the Philippine Islands invited us to preach at an evangelistic crusade in Pilar, in the northern province of Abra. The gospel had never been preached in this area. This particular zone was known to be controlled by the 'Guerillas' of the National People's Army (N.P.A.). Because this region was practically inaccessible, we needed a four wheel drive vehicle to get through unpaved roads, rivers, creeks, and mountainous areas. Two days prior to the crusade, a violent typhoon hit the area. The strong rains made access to this area impossible. Local pastors united to pray for a change in the weather. On the day of the crusade, we left for the region, rain and all. Ten minutes after starting out, the skies cleared and the sun shone with great brilliance. This, however, was just the beginning of our traveling struggles. An hour later we found that the road was closed due to a landslide. Once again, the local pastors began to intercede and in less than two hours the department of transportation had opened a way for our vehicles. According to many, this road-clearing job normally takes one to two days. Further along, while on a mountainous road, one of the jeeps hit a rock and broke the drive shaft. The local pastors suggested we continue in the other vehicle, while they walked the rest of the way; they were determined to hold these crusades in this unreached region.

While the worship team was unpacking their instruments, a vehicle descended from the mountains. More than ten armed men jumped out and surrounded us. After a few brief moments of conversation with the pastors in their native language, the men climbed in their vehicle and left. Pastor Lagmay's response to our excited questions was, "I told the 'Guerillas' that Felipe Delgado is an evangelist from Mexico and that you are from Colombia, and that you are here bringing the gospel of peace to this region. Hearing this they departed and allowed us to continue." The result of the crusades in Pilar, Abra was more than three hundred souls for Christ. At the end of the crusade, one of the pastors that came with us decided to permanently stay in Pilar and establish a local church. Two years later, I heard that the church was continuing to grow and that many of the 'Guerillas' had given their lives in service to the Lord. Without a doubt, all this was made possible because of intercessory prayers offered by the Filipino people which opened the doors of evangelism in that region.

SPIRITUAL WARFARE IN COLOMBIA, SOUTH AMERICA

On April 23-26, 1991, Dr. C. Peter Wagner and I were invited to hold a conference on spiritual warfare in Bogota, Colombia. This was possible through the invitation of the Evangelical Confederation of Colombia and the Evangelical Ministers Association. During this conference the ministerial body was challenged to unite in prayer to bind the spirits of violence and idolatry that existed in the nation in order to bring the nation to Christ. There was a genuine outpouring of love, and many of the pastors cried out to God to break the curses of past generations and for unity and love to be within the church. On April 25, Bogota's newspaper, El Tiempo, had on its first page an article entitled, 'Colombia will no longer be a Catholic nation.' The government had approved a constitutional amendment for religious freedom in the nation; this gave Christians access to mass media communication and recognition of their civil rights to practice their beliefs.

On April 26, we ended the conference by praying for peace and an end to the violence and drug trafficking caused by the Medellin Cartel. Approximately a month later, Larry Lea, the apostle of prayer, had an exciting meeting where thousands of people united and interceded for Colombia. Shortly thereafter, Pablo Escobar Gaviria, the leader of the Medellin

Cartel, and his followers turned themselves in to authorities, ending a time of violence in Medellin and ushering in a spiritual revival. Without a doubt, the prayers of the Colombian people brought down the seat of violence over this city. "And He said to them, 'I saw Satan fall like lightning from heaven." (Luke 10:18)

This was just the beginning of what God has in store for this nation. Shortly after that, the pastors of Santa Fe de Bogota became negligent with their call to unity, thus allowing the influence of the spirits of division and accusation to infiltrate their ranks under the guise of political differences. During the same time, Pablo Escobar Gaviria escaped from prison in Envigado and unleashed a new wave of terror that brought fear to the nation. Since that time an unprecedented spiritual awakening has taken place in that nation.

The prayer of intercession has had great impact in Latin-America. Many Presidents, Vice Presidents, Senators, Congressmen, and Councilmen are now evangelical men of God with a vision to impact and bring a positive change through the gospel in their nations.

Today, both the Medellin Cartel and the Cali Cartel have been totally dismantled. Today, the city of Cali is well known around the world for the total transformation of the community. The body of Christ has been holding three all-night prayer vigils a year in which as many as 65,000 people pray all night for their city and their nation. I have had the privilege of leading these multitudes in prayer, and on two occasions, the largest soccer stadium was filled to capacity.

Notes
[1] John Robb, From a report presented to the Spiritual Warfare Conference on November 1990, Pasadena California.

—————————◆—————————

CHAPTER SIXTEEN

PRAYER STRATEGIES

An intercessor is an imitator of Christ. Scripture teaches that He is at the right hand of God interceding for us. He lives to intercede for us. Every intercessor, whether male or female, young or old, is fighting for others. Dick Eastman, in his book *Love On Its Knees*, says that "prayer is not a battle weapon, but the battle itself. Prayer is the conflict by which the enemy is assaulted." [1]

Every intercessor recognizes that Satan has a specific strategy to attack Christians. Therefore, if Satan has a plan or a strategy, Christians need to be led by the Spirit and Word of God to develop and prepare a prayer strategy for the battle. "For by wise strategy you will wage war and in the abundance of counselors there is victory" (Proverbs 24:6).

> "Give ear to my words, O Lord, consider my medita-
> tion. Give heed to the voice of my cry, my King and
> my God, for to You I will pray. My voice You shall

hear in the morning, O Lord; in the morning I will direct it to You, and I will look up." (Psalm 5:1-3)

CHRISTIANS NEED TO BE LED BY
THE SPIRIT AND WORD OF GOD TO
DEVELOP AND PREPARE A PRAYER
STRATEGY FOR THE BATTLE

We need to develop a battle plan before venturing into the battle camp. No where in the Bible do we find room for confusion and disorganization. On the contrary, Paul exhorts us to "do everything decently and in order" (1 Corinthians 14:40 italics added).

What do we mean by 'strategy'? It is a plan of action. The Word of God gives us three foundational truths for victory in battle because "your adversary the devil walks about like a roaring lion, seeking whom he may devour" (I Peter 5:8). Here are three things you can do to begin your battle plan:

1. Self-control: Being sober. Being watchful of temptations against prayer.

2. Be alert: Vigilant. Sensitive to the voice of the Holy Spirit and the inner man.

3. Resist: Position yourself effectively. Attack the enemy. "Therefore submit to God. Resist the devil and he will flee from you. Draw near to God and He will draw near to you. Cleanse your hands, you sinners; and purify your hearts, you double-minded" (James 4:7-8).

As discussed in Chapter 14, the challenge to put on the whole armor of God and be strong in the Lord is a call to the prayer battle (Ephesians 6:10-18). These scriptures give us

the prayer instructions to be followed in intercessory warfare:
- ◆ Pray at all times
- ◆ Pray in the Spirit
- ◆ With all prayer and supplication
- ◆ Be alert
- ◆ Persevering in prayer for all the saints

Before spiritual warfare can be waged, we must know the following things:

1. Who is our enemy?
" For we wrestle not against flesh and blood, but against principalities, against powers, against the rulers of the darkness of this age, against spiritual hosts of wickedness in the heavenly places" (Ephesians 6:12).

2. What are our weapons?
" For though we walk in the flesh, we do not war according to the flesh. For the weapons of our warfare are not carnal but mighty in God for pulling down strongholds, casting down arguments and every high thing that exalts itself against the knowledge of God, bringing every thought into captivity to the obedience of Christ" (2 Corinthians 10:3-5). The weapons God has given us enable us to battle and pull down all strongholds in order to destroy the fortresses the enemy has built in all three levels of warfare.

a. Destroying or tearing down speculations (philosophical or ideological strongholds)

b. Destroying or tearing down every lofty thing (territorial strongholds)

c. Taking captive every thought (personal strongholds)

3. What is the strategy?
"For by wise strategy you will wage war. And in a multitude of counselors there is safety" (Proverbs 24:6).

4.   What is God's wisdom for the battle?

"Plans are established by counsel; by wise counsel wage war" (Proverbs 20:18).

"A wise man scales the city of the mighty, and brings down the trusted stronghold" (Proverbs 21:22).

"Wisdom is better than weapons of war; but one sinner destroys much good" (Ecclesiastes 9:18), or "One mistake can cause a lot of damage," Spanish Version Reina Valera, 1977 Revision.

This knowledge that is imparted to you **must** be used with divine wisdom. There is a great difference between knowledge and wisdom. Knowledge is that which we teach or learn from teaching. Wisdom is how this knowledge is used or applied. This is why I feel that knowledge without wisdom is dangerous. Paul states that knowledge 'puffs up' or brings pride, and pride leads to a downfall. Therefore we must be careful to observe and to do what we learn under the proper scrutiny and direction of those in authority, and certainly under a covering of "wise" counsel. As a Spanish Bible version reads, "Wisdom is better than weapons of war, for one mistake can cause a lot of damage."

Notes
[1] Eastman, p. 65.

———————◆———————

CHAPTER SEVENTEEN

PULLING DOWN STRONGHOLDS WITH INTERCESSION

Therefore humble yourselves under the mighty hand of God, that He may exalt you in due time, casting all your care upon Him, for He cares for you. Be sober, be vigilant; because your adversary the devil walks about like a roaring lion, seeking whom he may devour. Resist him, steadfast in the faith, knowing that the same sufferings are experienced by your brotherhood in the world. But may the God of all grace, who called us to His eternal glory by Christ Jesus, after you have suffered a while, perfect, establish, strengthen and settle you (1 Peter 5:6-10).

"Then He said to them, 'Nation will rise against nation, and kingdom against kingdom. And there will be great earthquakes in various places, and famines, and pestilences; and there will be fearful sights and great signs from heaven. But before all these things, they will lay their hands on you and persecute you, delivering you up to the synagogues and prisons. You will be brought before kings and rulers for My name's sake. But it will turn out for you as an occasion for testimony. Therefore settle it in your hearts, not to meditate beforehand on what you will answer; for I will give you a mouth and wisdom which all your adversaries will not be able to contradict or resist. You will be betrayed even by parents and brothers, relatives and friends; and they will put some of you to death. And you will be hated by all for My name's sake. But not a hair of your head shall be lost. By your patience possess your souls."   (Luke 21:10-19)

THIS IS TO SAY THAT INTERCESSION
SHOULD CONTINUE UNTIL WE SEE THE
TOTAL DESTRUCTION OF THE POWER OF
THE ENEMY OVER THE STRONGHOLD

God is raising up an army of believers with the purpose of uniting them in faith, love, and intercession. In this way, they will pull down strongholds, destroy the works of the enemy, bind the strong man, strip him of what he has stolen, and see the prophecies God has given which are to come to pass in the Church.

"This charge I commit to you, son Timothy, according to the prophecies previously made concerning you, that by them you may wage the good warfare, having faith and a good conscience, which some having rejected, concerning the faith have suffered shipwreck…" (1 Timothy 1:18-19)

"Fight the good fight of faith, lay hold on eternal life,
to which you were also called and have confessed the
good confession in the presence of many witnesses."
(1 Timothy 6:12)

The things that happen in the natural realm are the reflection and the result of what happens in the spiritual realm. We must learn to recognize the invisible world in order to identify what is happening in the natural. "For since the creation of the world His invisible attributes are clearly seen, being understood by the things that are made, even His eternal power and Godhead, so that they are without excuse" (Romans 1:20).

"…while we do not look at the things which are seen,
but at the things which are not seen. For the things
which are seen are temporary; but the things which
are not seen are eternal." (2 Corinthians 4:18)

This chapter focuses on the steps that are necessary in order to prepare a strategy for intercessory warfare.

RECOGNIZE TERRITORIAL SPIRITS

"... I lifted my eyes and looked, and behold, a certain man clothed in linen, whose waist was girded with gold of Uphaz! His body was like beryl, his face like the appearance of lightning, his eyes like torches of fire, his arms and feet like burnished bronze in color, and the sound of his words like the voice of a multitude. And I, Daniel, alone saw the vision; for the men who were with me did not see the vision .... Then he said to me, 'Do not fear, Daniel, for from the first day that you set your heart to understand, and to humble before your God, your words were heard; and I have come because of your words. But the prince of the kingdom of Persia withstood me twenty-one days; and behold, Michael, one of the chief princes, came to help me, for I had been left alone there with the kings of Persia. Now I have come to make you understand what will happen to your people in the latter days, for the vision refers to many days yet to come.' When he had spoken such words to me, I turned my face toward the ground and became speechless. ...Then he said, 'Do you know why I have come to you? And now I must return to fight with the prince of Persia, and when I have gone forth, indeed the prince of Greece will come. But I tell you what is noted in the scripture of Truth. No one upholds me against these, except Michael your prince'" (Daniel 10:5-7, 12-15, 20-21).

DISCERN THE GATES OF THE CITY: THERE ARE GATES OF LIGHT AND GATES OF DARKNESS

"And I also say to you that you are Peter, and on this rock I will build My Church, and the gates of Hades shall not prevail against it." (Matthew 16:18)

"And he was afraid and said, 'How awesome is this place! This is none other than the house of God, and this is the gate of heaven!.'" (Genesis 28:17)

"Those from among you shall build the old waste places; ...and you shall be called the Repairer of the Breach, the Restorer of Streets to dwell in." (Isaiah 58:12)

"When a strong man, fully armed, guards his own palace, his goods are in peace. But when a stronger than he comes upon him and overcomes him, he takes from him all his armor in which he trusted, and divides his spoils." (Luke 11:21)

RECOGNIZE CORPORATE SIN

That is to say, assume responsibility for the sins of our towns, our nations, and our congregation as if they were our own sins.

"And I said: 'I pray, Lord God of heaven, O great and awesome God, You who keep Your covenant and mercy with those who love You and observe Your commandments, please let Your ear be attentive and Your eyes open, that You may hear the prayer of Your servant which I pray before You now, day and night, for the children of Israel Your servants, and confess the sins of the children of Israel which we have sinned against You. Both my father's house and I have sinned. We have acted very corruptly against You, and have not kept the commandments, the statutes, nor the ordinances which You commanded Your servant Moses" (Nehemiah 1:5-7).

"Then I set my face toward the Lord God to make request by prayer and supplications, with fasting, sackcloth, and ashes. And I prayed to the Lord my God, and made confession, and said, 'O Lord, great and awesome God, who keeps His covenant and mercy with those who love Him, and with those who keep His commandments, we have sinned and committed iniquity, we have done wickedly and rebelled, even by departing from Your precepts and Your judgments. Neither have we heeded Your servants the prophets, who spoke in Your name to our kings and our princes, to our fathers and all the people of the land. O Lord, righteousness belongs to You, but to us shame of face, as it is this day — to the men of Judah, to the inhabitants of Jerusalem and all Israel, those near and those far off in all the countries to which You have driven them, because of the unfaithfulness which they have committed against You. O Lord, to us belongs shame of face, to our kings, our princes, and our fathers, because we have sinned against You. To the Lord our God belong mercy and forgiveness, though we have rebelled against Him. We have not obeyed the voice of the Lord our God, to walk in His laws, which He set before us by His servants the prophets. Yes, all Israel has transgressed Your law, and has departed so as not to obey Your voice; therefore the curse and the oath written in the Law of Moses the servant of God have been poured out on us, because we have sinned against Him.   O Lord, according to all Your righteousness, I pray, let Your anger and Your fury be turned away from Your city Jerusalem, Your holy mountain; because for our sins, and for the iniquities of our fathers, Jerusalem and Your people are a reproach to all those around us. Now therefore, our God, hear the prayer of Your servant, and his supplications, and for the Lord's sake cause Your face to shine on Your sanctuary, which is desolate. O my God, incline Your ear and hear; open Your eyes and see our desolation, and the city which is called by Your name; for we do not present our supplications before You because of our righteous deeds, but because of Your great mercies. O Lord, hear! O Lord, forgive! O Lord, listen and act!" (Daniel 9:3-12, 16-19a)

LEARN TO PRAY AND INTERCEDE IN ACCORDANCE WITH THE WORD OF GOD

When we try to manipulate God by means of prayer, we are operating in witchcraft (occult). Manipulation and control are the foundation of the kingdom of darkness. For example: "God, make this man marry me," or "God, remove and take away this person from the church," etc.

What is the difference between prayer and intercession? All intercession is prayer; but not all prayer is intercession. When interceding you pray for others. You become their shield of protection against the enemy's attacks. This means the enemy can counterattack you. Intercession involves pulling down strongholds that the enemy has built and destroying the works of the enemy by casting down territorial spirits (e.g., idolatry, pride, occult, immorality) which brings victory to the kingdom of God. Intercession often is manifested through tears, pain, laughter, shouts, etc.

Strongholds are not destroyed (on many occasions) for various reasons, including:

♦   The intercessors have not prayed specifically and in unity against the powers behind these strongholds. Their prayers have been scattered instead of hitting the 'bulls eye.' Sometimes the prayers may weaken the strongholds, but they do not destroy them, so they remain in control. If there isn't a unanimous request for forgiveness of the sins that gave authority and right for demons to operate, they will return with much more power.

♦   Often we win battles, but not the war, because we don't fight to the end. We leave things half way done, thus allowing the enemy to regain new strength.

"'Is not My word like a fire?' says the Lord, 'And like a hammer that breaks the rock in pieces'" (Jeremiah 23:29)?

Occasionally the strike of the hammer will weaken, but a continuous and steady blow will break the strongholds to pieces. This is to say that intercession should continue until we see the total destruction of the power of the enemy over the stronghold. The plan of resistance requires the following:

1. Recognize the enemy
2. Discern the spirits
3. Plan the strategy
4. Attack strongholds until they are totally destroyed. "See, I have this day set you over the nations and over the kingdoms, to root out and to pull down, to destroy and to throw down, to build and to plant" (Jeremiah 1:10).

> "Please forgive the trespass of your maidservant. For the Lord will certainly make for my lord an enduring house, because my lord fights the battles of the Lord, and evil is not found in you throughout your days."
> (1 Samuel 25:28)

The Church in the western world has fallen under the influence of philosophies and thinkers that deny the supernatural and only believe and accept those things for which they can find scientific or rational explanations. The apostle Paul very wisely stated, "But the natural man does not receive things of the Spirit of God, for they are foolishness to him; nor can he know them, because they are spiritually discerned" (1 Corinthians 2:14).

---◆---

CHAPTER EIGHTEEN

PULLING DOWN STRONGHOLDS WITH FASTING

And when He had come into the house, His disciples asked Him privately, 'Why could we not cast it out?' So He said to them, 'This kind can come out by nothing but prayer and fasting' (Mark 9:28-29).

When we are interceding and battling against the powers of darkness, sometimes it may be necessary to reinforce our prayers with a fast. Fasting and prayer are related. Fasting gives a supernatural power and an added push to our prayers. Intercession is a denial of oneself in order to focus one's prayer for others. Fasting is a denial of one's flesh to give emphasis to one's prayer, giving it more power. As we combine prayer and fasting, we enter into the highest level of prayer because it increases our sensitivity to the guidance of the Holy Spirit. Prayer and fasting make you more sensitive to the voice of God. Fasting is the deliberate practice of voluntarily abstaining from the usual nutrition of food and drink. When we fast, we humble ourselves before God, and this allows us to have a greater sensibility to the things of God as we 'die' to the flesh. David states in Psalm 69:10a: *"When I wept and chastened my soul with fasting."* The new English version says, *"I humbled my spirit with fasting"* (italics added).

Fasting is a dying to the flesh and the spirit. This should encourage us to avoid spiritual pride and the 'pharisaism' Jesus called hypocrisy. "Moreover, when you fast, do not be like the hypocrites, with a sad countenance. For they disfigure their faces that they may appear to men to be fasting. Assuredly, I say to you, they have their reward. But you, when you fast, anoint your head and wash your face, so that you do not appear to men to be fasting, but to your Father who is in the secret place; and your Father who sees in secret will reward you openly" (Matthew 6: 16-18).

Fasting is a commitment before God of having self-control (temperance) over the passion for food and one's appetite; that is to say, to mortify or put to death that which is impure and excessive. The Psalmist says in *Psalm 35* that he was subjugating his body with prayer and fasting, praying for his enemies with all of his heart. This is what Paul is referring to in 1 Corinthians 9:27 when he says that he disciplines his body and brings it into subjection that it (the body) may learn to do what it should, not what it (the body) wants.

Fasting increases our sensitivity to the voice of the Holy Spirit. "As they ministered to the Lord and fasted, the Holy Spirit said,'Now separate to Me Barnabas and Paul for the work to which I have called them.' Then having fasted and prayed, and laid hands on them, they sent them away" (Acts 13:2-3).

Notice that verse two says *"then having fasted and prayed."* This demonstrates that worship is a form of praying. The disciples saw the value of fasting in order to hear from God.

Prayer and fasting bring God's protection. "Then I proclaimed a fast there at the river of Ahava, that we might humble ourselves before our God, to seek from Him the right way for us and our little ones and all our possessions. For I was ashamed to request of the king an escort of soldiers and horsemen to help us against the enemy on the road, because we had spoken to the king, saying, 'The hand of our God is upon all those for good who seek Him, but His power and His wrath are against all those who forsake Him.' So we fasted and entreated our God for this, and He answered our prayer" (Ezra 8:21-23).

"'...strengthening the souls of the disciples, exhorting them to continue in the faith,' and saying, 'We must through many tribulations enter the Kingdom of God.' So when they had appointed elders in every church, and prayed with fasting, they commended them to the Lord in whom they had believed." (Acts 14:22-23)

Fasting empowers us with the power of the Holy Spirit. The Bible tells us in Luke 4 that "Jesus returned in the power of the Holy Spirit to Galilee." He had been 40 days without eating. Jesus' fast was abstaining from solid foods, not from water or liquids. Jesus Christ was taken into the desert having the power of God internally, but He came out empowered by the manifestation of the Holy Spirit. During this fast Satan tempted Jesus with all manner of temptation and departed from Him until a later time.

How then should we fast? We need to begin with wisdom. Though the Bible makes mention of prolonged fasts (three, seven, twenty-one, and forty days), more frequently it reveals fasts of less than twenty-four hours.

"'Why have we fasted,' they say, 'and You have not seen? Why have we afflicted our souls, and You take no notice?' 'In fact, in the day of your fast you find pleasure, and exploit all your laborers. Indeed you fast for strife and debate, and to strike with the fist of wickedness. You will not fast as you do this day, to make your voice heard on high. Is it a fast that I have chosen, a day for a man to afflict his soul? Is it to bow down his head like a bulrush, and to spread out sack-cloth and ashes? Would you call this a fast, and an acceptable day to the Lord? Is this not the fast that I have chosen: to loose the bonds of wickedness, to undo the heavy burdens, to let the oppressed go free, and that you break every yoke? Is it not to share your bread with the hungry, and that you bring to your house the poor who are cast out; when you see the naked, that you cover him, and not hide yourself from your own flesh? Then your light shall break forth like the morn-ing, your healing shall spring forth speedily, and your righteousness shall go before you; the glory of the Lord shall be your rear guard. Then you shall call, and the Lord will answer; You shall cry, and He will say, 'Here I am.'" (Isaiah 58:3-9)

———————————————◆———————————————

AS WE COMBINE PRAYER AND FASTING, WE ENTER INTO THE HIGHEST LEVEL OF PRAYER BECAUSE IT INCREASES OUR SENSITIVITY TO THE GUIDANCE OF THE HOLY SPIRIT

———————————————◆———————————————

The Church of Acts transformed the world because they were disciplined to the power of prayer and fasting. "So Cornelius said, 'Four days ago I was fasting until this hour; and at the ninth hour I prayed in my house, and behold a man stood before me in bright clothing...'" (Acts 10:30).

"As they ministered to the Lord and fasted, the Holy Spirit said, 'Now separate to Me Barnabas and Saul for the work to which I have called them.'" (Acts 13:2)

"So when they had appointed elders in every church, and prayed with fasting, they commended them to the Lord in whom they had believed." (Acts 14:23)

Paul was a person that fasted continually in the exercise of his ministry (1 Corinthians 11:27). Dr. Kingsley Fletcher writes in his wonderful book *Prayer and Fasting,* "Without prayer and fasting our faith cannot function. Without prayer and fasting, some miracles will never happen, some circumstances will never change, some situations will never be reversed. Prayer and fasting sharpen your expectancy so that when you ask, you expect to receive."[1]

Fasting is part of the discipline required for spiritual warfare because it makes us stronger and tougher physically, mentally, and emotionally.

Notes
[1] Dr. Kingsley Fletcher, *Prayer and Fasting.* Shippensburg PA: Destiny Image Publishing, 1992, p.33.

---◆---

CHAPTER NINETEEN

PULLING DOWN STRONGHOLDS WITH PRAISE AND WORSHIP

I want to make it clear that we praise God for His deeds and we worship Him for who He is: His character and His glory. We can say that praise is giving honor and glory as well as magnifying God. Worship literally means to kiss (*pros-kuneo*) and it is used when giving homage, reverence, and veneration to someone or something. Worship not only refers to singing and giving thanks; worship also involves action that recognizes God for His nature and His attributes.

> "Your hands have made me and fashioned me; give me understanding, that I may learn Your commandments." (Psalm 119:73)

> "Everyone who is called by My name, whom I have created for My glory; I have formed him, yes, I have made him." (Isaiah 43:7)

God made man with the ability to praise Him. Praise and worship is part of every human being's nature. Therefore, a person does not decide whether or not to praise or worship God, but rather *how* to praise and worship God.

God demands total adoration from His children (those that are called by His name) and that they only worship Him. Men have chosen to worship their jobs, their families, their material possessions, their riches, their appearance, etc., yet there is a biblical principal that states that man is a servant of what he worships. Worship and serving go hand in hand. We cannot separate one from the other.

> "Again, the devil took Him up on an exceeding high mountain, and showed Him all the kingdoms of the world and their glory. And he said to Him, 'All these things I will give You if You will fall down and worship me'. Then Jesus said to him 'Away with you, Satan! For it is written, you shall worship the Lord your God and Him only you shall serve.'" (Matthew 4:8-10)

WHEREVER THE SPIRIT OF WORSHIP
IS, WITH GOD ENTHRONED AND
EXALTED, NEITHER FLESH NOR
DEMON CAN CARRY OUT THEIR PURPOSES

"But the hour is coming, and now is, when the true worshippers will worship the Father in spirit and truth; for the Father is seeking such to worship Him. God is Spirit, and those who worship Him must worship in spirit and truth" (John 4:23-24). "In spirit" refers to worship that comes from deep within our being. "In truth" refers to absolute honesty and transparency before God, hiding nothing. It can also mean to worship in "tongues" and in truth, proclaiming, confessing, and singing the Word of God which is the real Truth.

YOU HAVE ESTABLISHED STRENGTH

"Enter into His gates with thanksgiving, and into His courts with praise. Be thankful to Him, and bless His name" (Psalm 100:4). When we begin to praise God, we open the door to His courts, thus giving God the opportunity to pour out a blessing on us or miraculously work on our behalf. Worship brings us into the very presence of the Most High, into the Holy of Holies, allowing God's glory to be made manifest and bring victory, healing, and liberation. David understood this spiritual dimension and he knew how to use it to battle against his enemies. Goliath wasn't destroyed because of David's strength and ability, but because David was praising and exalting God.

"O, Lord, our Lord, how excellent is Your name in all the earth, who have set Your glory above the heavens! Out of the mouth of babes and nursing infants You have ordained strength, because of Your enemies, that You may silence the enemy and the avenger." (Psalm 8:1-2)

"But when the chief priests and scribes saw the wonderful things that He did, and the children crying out in the temple and saying, 'Hosanna to the Son of the David!' They were indignant and said to Him, 'Do You hear what these are saying?' And Jesus said to them, 'Yes, have you never read, Out of the mouth of babes and nursing infants you have perfected praise?'" (Matthew 21:15-16)

You Have Prepared Praise.

Praise and strength are synonymous to God. This is why scripture declares, *"...the joy (cheerfulness, praise) of the Lord is your strength"* (Nehemiah 8:10 italics added).

Note what Jesus teaches regarding the mouth. The mouth is the vehicle by which we can use the weapons for warfare. Revelation 16:13 says that "out of the mouth of the dragon, out of the mouth of the beast and out of the mouth of the false prophet" came demonic spirits for the battle. In the same manner, God's weapons are used by means of the mouth: by proclaiming, praising, shouting, declaring, and confessing the Lord. "Save us, O Lord our God, and gather us from among the Gentiles, to give thanks to Your holy name, to triumph in Your praise" (Psalm 106:47).

The triumph is in the praise. There's a difference between triumph and victory. Victory is the defeat of the enemy. Triumph is the celebration of the victory already obtained. 2 Corinthians 2:14 states that when praise is given we can see the manifestation of the power of God and of His salvation.

You Are Fearful in Praises

"Who is like You, O Lord, among the gods? Who is like You, glorious in holiness, fearful in praises, doing wonder? You stretched out Your right hand; the earth swallowed them." (Exodus 15:11-12)

♦ Joshua had a victory in Jericho. When the people praised God with shouts of praise and the sound of trumpets, then the walls came tumbling down.
♦ David destroyed Goliath because he exalted and praised God.

♦ Jehoshaphat saw Jehovah's victory because the people began to praise God, singing songs of worship and praise, and "the Lord set ambushes against the enemy's armies."

♦ Paul and Silas were freed from prison chains because they prayed and sang praises to God. The Word says that "suddenly there was a great earthquake…and immediately all the doors were opened and everyone's chains were loosed."

> "Now these are the men whom David appointed over the service of song in the house of the Lord, after the ark came to rest. They were ministering with music before the dwelling place of the tabernacle of meeting, until Solomon had built the house of the Lord in Jerusalem and they served in their office according to their order."   (1 Chronicles 6:31-32)

"These are the singers, heads of the fathers' houses of the Levites, who lodged in the chambers, and were free from other duties; for they were employed in that work day and night" (1 Chronicles 9:33). The singers were a permanent part of the temple services. The music ministers worked full-time and received a salary and tithes from the people. This would indicate to us the importance of music in our celebrations. Music in a worship service is not a warm-up exercise, nor a time-killer, nor is it used to wait for late-comers. It is not a display of our talents, nor is it a tool for evangelism. It is to praise and worship God.

The armies of the world march to battle accompanied with music; God's army should do the same. We must emphasize that the stronger the battle, the more we should sing and praise the Lord. Music is the means of expression that the Church has towards its Love. It is like a serenade that brings the Lord's blessing and favor with songs of deliverance.

"You are my hiding place; You shall preserve me from trouble; You shall surround me with songs of deliverance." (Psalm 32:7) God wants to break chains with songs of deliverance that destroy walls and bring healing. *"I am the God that heals you"* (Exodus 15:26 italics added).

Pastor Jack Hayford of Church On the Way in Van Nays, California, stated that "Worship has the power to neutralize the enemy's forces over God's people. Wherever the spirit of worship is, with God enthroned and exalted, neither flesh nor demon can carry out their purposes."

> "Let the saints be joyful in glory; let them sing aloud on their beds. Let the high praises of God be in their mouth, and a two-edged sword in their hand, to execute vengeance on the nations, and punishments on the peoples; to bind their kings with chains, and their nobles with fetters of iron; to execute on them the written judgement—this honor have all His saints. Praise the Lord!"   (Psalm 149:5-9)

———————◆———————

CHAPTER TWENTY

PULLING DOWN STRONGHOLDS WITH THE NAME OF JESUS

Our weapons are not human; they are divinely powerful to destroy and demolish strongholds."For though we walk in the flesh, we do not war according to the flesh. For the weapons of our warfare are not carnal but mighty in God for pulling down strongholds." (2 Corinthians 10:3-4)

"Even to them I will give in My house and within My walls a place and a name better than that of sons and daughters; I will give them an everlasting name that shall not be cut off. Also the sons of the foreigner who join themselves to the Lord, to serve Him, and to love the name the name of the Lord, to be His servants – everyone who keeps from defiling the Sabbath, and holds fast My covenant – even them I will bring to My holy mountain, and make them joyful in My house of prayer. Their burnt offerings and their sacrifices will be accepted on My altar; for My house shall be called a house of prayer for all nations." (Isaiah 56:5-7)

The book of Hebrews tells us that Jesus Christ is far more superior to the angels for he "inherited a more excellent name." There are three ways to inherit or use a name:

1.   Through birth (the Church).   We are born into the family of God through Jesus Christ who is the living and abiding Word of God, from the seed (gr. sperma) of our Heavenly Father.   "Having been born again, not of corruptible seed but incorruptible, through the word of God which lives and abides forever" (1 Peter 1.23).   This 'seed' to which the text refers is the creative word of God which is 'conceived' in our hearts through faith and causes a regeneration in our spirits. The end result is our new spiritual birth. The word 'incorruptible' is really the Greek word for *immortal*; in other words, *eternal life.*

2.   Through adoption (Israel).   Most Christian circles teach that the Christian believer is *adopted* into God's family. The scriptures plainly indicate that the *adoption* belongs to the people of Israel or the Jew. Paul plainly states: "For I could wish that I myself were accursed from Christ for my brethren, my countrymen according to the flesh, who are Israelites, to whom pertain the adoption, the glory, the covenants, the giving of the law, the service of God and the promises" (Romans 9. 4-5).

3.   Through power (an official authority that grants the power to use someone else's name and signature).   In the business world this is called a *power of attorney.*   What value, what power, what significance is there in the use of a name? This all depends on the power, the authority that the name represents.   Is there power in the name of Jesus?

"Therefore God also has highly exalted Him and given

Him the name which is above every name, that at the name of Jesus every knee should bow, of those in heaven, and of those on earth, and of those under the earth, and that every tongue should confess that Jesus Christ is Lord, to the glory of God the Father." (Philippians 2:9-11)

A NAME ABOVE ALL NAMES

God gave Jesus a name that is above every other name; a name that has authority over all things, visible and invisible.
"And these signs, will follow those who believe: In My name they will cast out demons; they will speak with new tongues; they will take up serpents; and if they drink anything deadly it will by no means hurt them; they will lay hands on the sick, and they will recover."   (Mark 16:17-18)

In the name of Jesus, there is authority over demons, sicknesses, principalities, powers, and strongholds, both visible and invisible. When we are born into the family of God, our salvation begins by the authority and power of His name. "Nor is there salvation in any other, for there is no other name under heaven given among men by which we must be saved" (Acts 4:12).

The word salvation *(soteria)* denotes the following: spiritual freedom, financial freedom, and emotional deliverance. It can also be translated to mean preservation, liberty, and health. The name of Jesus has been given to us by God's grace so that salvation can be offered to all men. The name of Jesus (Greek) is the same as Joshua (Hebrew, *Jehoshua)* and means Jehovah, or "Yahweh is savior," so Joshua means savior.

"And when they had set them in the midst, they asked, 'By what power or by what name have you done this?'" (Acts 4:7) The question was, "What power or authority do you have; in what name or in whose name do you work?" "And whatever you ask in My name, that I will do, that the Father may be glorified in the Son. If you ask anything in My name, I will do it" (John 14:13-14).

> "And in that day you will ask Me nothing. Most assuredly, I say to you, whatever you ask the Father in My name He will give you. Until now you have asked nothing in My name. Ask, and you will receive, that your joy may be full." (John 16:23-24)

> "Now, Lord, look on their threats, and grant to Your servants that with all boldness they may speak Your Word by stretching out Your hand to heal, and that signs and wonders may be done through the name of Your holy Servant Jesus. And when they had prayed, the place where they were assembled together was shaken; and they were all filled with the Holy Spirit, and they spoke the Word of God with boldness." (Acts 4:29-31)

POWER IN THE NAME OF JESUS

The name of Jesus makes all hell tremble. When we call on the name of Jesus, we are calling on all of Heaven's resources. In the spiritual realm, the name of the Living Word is the seal that authorizes the written word to be manifested in the natural realm. When we declare God's promises, when we ask the Father in Jesus' name, we have immediate access to heaven's resources.

"Now it happened, as we went to prayer, that a certain slave girl possessed with a spirit of divination met us, who brought her masters much profit by fortune-telling. This girl followed Paul and us, and cried out, saying, 'These men are the servants of the Most High God, who proclaim to us the way of salvation.' And this she did for many days. But Paul, greatly annoyed, turned and said to the spirit, 'I command you in the name of Jesus Christ to come out of her.' And he came out that very hour." (Acts 16:16-18)

"Therefore I say to you, whatever things you ask when you pray, believe that you receive them, and you will have them. And whenever you stand praying, if you have anything against anyone, forgive him, that your Father in heaven may also forgive you your trespasses. But if you do not forgive, neither will your Father in heaven forgive your trespasses." (Mark 11:24-26)

AUTHORITY IN THE NAME OF JESUS

"...All authority has been given to Me in heaven and on earth" (Matthew 28:18). God has given the name of Jesus to us as a weapon. It gives us authority. "Nor is there salvation in any other, for there is no other name under heaven given among men by which we must be saved" (Acts 4:12).

To the early church, the name of Jesus had great significance. It was part of its ministry. Today, secular educators do not want the name of Jesus to be mentioned in schools. Mohammed, Buddha, the Pope, Krishna, etc. may be named, but when the Bible, Christian, or Jesus is named, all persecution alarms go off. Why? Because Satan and his evil powers fear the name of Jesus! Acts 9:16 says that we will suffer for

His name's sake. Matthew 10:22 says that we will be hated because of His name.

Matthew 24 speaks of the end time signs. Matthew 24:9 tells us of one of the signs before His coming: "Then they will deliver you up to tribulation and kill you, and you will be hated by all nations for My name's sake."

There is so much power and authority in Jesus' name that all of hell's weapons are aimed against those that believe, confess, and use the name of Jesus. Thousands come against the name of Jesus of Nazareth. When we are shamed because of the name of Jesus, we should rejoice because the glory of God's Spirit rests upon us. There is power and authority in the name of Jesus. When you use the name of Jesus in battle, you must do so with the knowledge that God has given Him authority over every other name. The name of Jesus opens doors in the spirit realm.

WHEN YOU USE THE NAME OF JESUS IN BATTLE, YOU MUST DO SO WITH THE KNOWLEDGE THAT GOD HAS GIVEN HIM AUTHORITY OVER EVERY OTHER NAME

When we pray using the name of Jesus, in accordance with scripture, according to the will of God, with knowledge and wisdom, it is as if Jesus Christ Himself is praying. There isn't a power, stronghold, or authority in heaven, on earth, or in hell that could detain God from confirming His Word (John 14:13). God backs up the name of Jesus with His integrity and His omnipotence. All of God's power is available to all that invoke the name of Jesus. Satan does not dare confront the soldier who is dressed with God's justice and who knows, recognizes, and uses that great name.

The power of God is not only found in long prayers and fasting, but also in learning how to use God's weapons according to His Word and in the power of the Holy Spirit. This is what makes the enemy tremble.

"Now John answered Him, saying, 'Teacher, we saw someone who does not follow us casting out demons in Your name, and we forbade him because he does not follow us.' But Jesus said, 'Do not forbid him, for no one who works a miracle in My name can soon afterward speak evil of Me.'"   (Mark 9:38-39)

SALVATION IN THE NAME OF JESUS

"Now when He was in Jerusalem at the Passover, during the feast, many believed in His name when they saw the signs which He did." (John 2:23)

"He who believes in Him is not condemned; already, because he has not believed in the name of the only begotten Son of God." (John 3:18)

"And those who know Your name will put their trust in You; for You, Lord, have not forsaken those who seek You." (Psalm 9:10)

How great is the Lord's name in all the earth! Call on the name of the Lord because everyone who calls on His name shall be saved!

◆───────────────◆

CHAPTER TWENTY ONE

PULLING DOWN STRONGHOLDS WITH GOD'S ANGELS

For He shall give His angels charge over you, To keep you in all your ways. In their hands they shall bear you up, lest you dash your foot against a stone. (Psalm 91.11-12)

Dr. Billy Graham, in his best-selling book *Angels*, writes "The enemies of Christ who attack us incessantly would often be thwarted if we could grasp God's assurance that His mighty angels are always nearby, ready to help. Tragically, most Christians have failed to accept this fact so frequently expressed in the Bible. I have noticed, though, that in my travels the closer I get to the frontiers of the Christian faith the more faith in angels I find among believers. Hundreds of stories document extraordinary divine intervention every year: God is using His angels as ministering spirits." [1]

"But to which of the angels has He ever said: 'Sit at My right hand, till I make Your enemies Your footstool?' Are they not all ministering spirits sent forth to minister for those who will inherit salvation?" (Hebrews 1:13-14)

Before entering into battle, we must be equipped and trained with the necessary weapons. Also we need to have the needed strategy and maturity to survive the attacks of the enemy. The battle has begun. God's army needs to know the weapons available to it in order to face the enemy. So then, let us consider and pay attention to these truths. Let's allow them to penetrate our hearts because, at this very moment, we are in the presence of many angels.

> "For to which of the angels did He ever say: 'You are My Son, today I have begotten You?' And again: 'I will be to Him a Father, and He shall be to Me a Son?' But when He again brings the firstborn into the world, He says: 'Let all the angels of God worship Him.' And of the angels He says: 'Who makes His angels spirits and His ministers a flame of fire.'"
> (Hebrews 1:5-7)

> "... For if the word spoken through angels proved steadfast, and every transgression and disobedience received a just reward, how shall we escape if we neglect so great a salvation, which at the first began to be spoken by the Lord, and was confirmed to us by those who heard Him, God also bearing witness both with signs and wonders, with various miracles, and gifts of the Holy Spirit, according to His own will?"
> (Hebrews 2:1-4)

MESSENGERS OF GOD

Angels are God's messengers. The Greek term *'angeloi'* means messengers or emissaries of God. They are spiritual beings that battle for God and His children. They don't dress in white, they do not have wings, nor are they effeminate as they are often depicted in works of art. On the contrary, these beings guard and represent God's best interests. In Revelation 5:11 we read that the number of angels is millions of millions. Job 38:7 states that the angels shouted with joy when God created the heavens and the earth.

In the *Institutes of the Christian Religion, 1,* John Calvin wrote, "The angels are the dispensers and administrators of the divine beneficence toward us; they regard our safety, undertake our defense, direct our ways, and exercise a constant solicitude that no evil befall us."

Angels appear in human form as we see in the incident with Lot when he lived in Sodom and Gomorrah. Angels arrived at his home to warn him of the coming destruction and the need to flee.

> "'Therefore I came without objection as soon as I was sent for. I ask, then, for what reason have you sent for me?' So Cornelius said, 'Four days ago I was fasting until this hour; and at the ninth hour I prayed in my house, and behold, a man stood before me in bright clothing, and said, "Cornelius, your prayer has been heard, and your alms are remembered in the sight of God. Send therefore to Joppa and call Simon here, whose surname is Peter. He is lodging in the house of Simon, a tanner, by the sea. When he comes, he will speak to you." So I sent to you immediately, and you have done will to come." (Acts 10:29-35a)

> "Let brotherly love continue. Do not forget to entertain strangers, for by so doing some have unwittingly entertained angels." (Hebrews 13:1-2)

In his book, *Taking Our Cities for God,* John Dawson has a chapter entitled, "All About Angels." Here he explains in detail the ministry of angels and the numerous biblical references to ministering angels. [2] They are spoken of as being masculine, but they do not marry or reproduce. They are an army, a company, and not a race. Among angels, there are those who represent different functions and positions of authority. They include thrones, dominions, powers or authorities, cherubim, archangels, and guardian angels. Matthew 18:10 tells us that "their" angels (talking about children) always see the face of "my Father who is in heaven." Angels celebrate. Luke 15:7 says "there is joy in heaven over one sinner who repents."

ANGELS AND CHRISTIANS ARE ALLIED IN THE BATTLE AGAINST SATAN

Angels are commissioned to execute divine judgment over people, cities, and nations. "And the people kept shouting, 'The voice of a god and not of a man!' Then immediately an angel of the Lord struck him, because he did not give glory to God. And he was eaten by worms and died" (Acts 12:22-23).

"On the twenty-fourth day of the eleven month, which is the month Shebat, in the second year of Darius, and the word of the Lord came to Zechariah the son of Berechiah, the son of Iddo the prophet: I saw by night, and behold, a man riding on a red horse, and it stood among the myrtle trees in the hollow; and behind him were horses: Red, sorrel, and white. Then I said, 'My lord, what are these?' So the angel who talked with me said to me, 'I will show you what they are.'" (Zechariah 1:7-9)

Angels should not be worshipped since they are our fellow servants. Only God should be worshipped. "And I fell at his feet to worship him. But he said to me, 'See that you do not do that! I am your fellow servant, and of your brethren who have the testimony of Jesus. Worship God.'" (Revelation 19:10)

"Let no one cheat you of your reward, taking delight in false humility and worship of angels, intruding into those things which he has not seen, vainly puffed up be his fleshly mind,..." (Colossians 2:18)

The Word says that we will judge the angels. Paul exhorts us saying that even *"..if we, or an angel from heaven preach any other gospel to you than what we have preached to you, let him be accursed"* (Galatians 1:8 italics added).

ANGELS ASSIST US IN SPIRITUAL BATTLE

"Every true believer in Christ should be encouraged and strengthened! Angels are watching; they make our path. They superintend the events of our lives and protect the interest of the Lord God, always working to promote His plans to bring about His highest will for us. Angels are interested spectators and mark all we do, 'for we are made a spectacle unto the world, and to angels, and to men' (1 Corinthians 4:9). God assigns angelic powers to watch over us." [3]

Angels and Christians are allied in the battle against Satan. Through intercessory prayers, angels are immediately dispatched to assist us with our requests before the Lord.

For those interested in the topic of angels, Dr. Gary Kinnaman, Senior Pastor of Word of Grace Church in Mesa,

AZ, has written an outstanding book called *Angels Dark and Light*. Published by Servant Publications, this has become a best seller. [4]

Notes

[1] Billy Graham, *Angels*. Waco TX: Word Publishing, 1975, p. 135.

[2] John Dawson, *Taking Our Cities for God*. Orlando FL: Creation House, 1989.

[3] Graham, p. 141.

[4] Gary Kinnaman, *Angels Dark and Light*. Grand Rapids MI: Chosen Books, 1994.

PART SIX

---◆---

THE CONFLICT

"Blessed be the Lord my Rock, Who trains my hands for war, And my fingers for battle." (Psalm 144:1)

———————◆———————

CHAPTER TWENTY TWO

VULNERABLE AREAS IN SPIRITUAL BATTLE

Our adversary (enemy, opponent), the devil, is seeking whom and how he may devour. He seeks vulnerable areas, weak areas, areas in which we are prone to suffer injury or defeat. *"Be sober, be vigilant; because your adversary the devil walks about like a roaring lion, seeking whom he may devour"* (1 Peter 5:8 italics added).

There are five areas in which the enemy works to destroy the immediate family and the Church:

RELATIONSHIPS

The enemy tries to destroy relationships between Christian brothers and the immediate family.

"And in the process of time it came to pass that Cain brought an offering of the fruit of the ground to the Lord. Abel also brought of the firstborn of his flock and of their fat. And the Lord respected Abel and his offering, but He did not respect Cain and his offering. And Cain was very angry, and his countenance fell. So the Lord said to Cain, 'Why are you so angry? And why has your countenance fallen? If you do well, will you not be accepted? And if you do not do well, sin lies at the door. And its desire is for you, but you should rule over it.'" (Genesis 4:3-8)

Jealousy, envy, and the spirit of accusation are the greatest weapons for division. The enemy uses this spirit of accusation to bring discord, division, and doubt against our leaders and brothers. When this happens we can be sure it is not from God. God is not the author of confusion, but of peace. Satan can use holy vessels to interfere with God's plan.

"Then Peter took Him aside and began to rebuke Him, saying, 'Far be it from You, Lord; this shall not happen to You!' But He turned and said to Peter, 'Get behind Me, Satan! You are an offense to Me, for you are not mindful of the things of God, but the things of men.'" (Matthew 16:22-23)

The spirit of accusation and slander has caused discouragement, division, and hurt. For the most part, accusations are directed towards those that are in leadership positions. This is why we must have better personal relationships and rebuke every spirit of accusation and criticism. Stop Satan immediately! For he is known as the accuser and slanderer of the brethren. "Then I heard a loud voice saying in heaven, 'Now salvation;, and strength, and the kingdom of our God, and the power of His Christ have come, for the accuser of our brethren, who accused them before our God day and night, has been cast down'" (Revelation 12:10).

These same spirits are seen in the home. They incite accusations and slander among husbands and wives, brothers and sisters, parents, and children, etc. "Out of the same mouth proceed blessing and cursing. My brethren, these things ought not to be so" (James 3:10).

FINANCES

This is a very delicate and sensitive area. We have to be careful and wise to avoid manipulation and abuse of kindness under the pretext of needs. We must be very sensitive to those in need. We need to pray for them, teach them, advise them, and meet the need when necessary. We need to strengthen one another in God's love.

> "If a brother or sister is naked and destitute of daily food, and one of you says to them, 'Depart in peace, be warmed and filled,' but you do not give them the things which are needed for the body, what does it profit?" (James 2:15-16)

> "For even when we were with you, we commanded you this: If anyone will not work, neither shall he eat." (II Thessalonians 3:10)

FAMILY

We need to constantly fight for the members of our family, praying for them, giving support, discipline, and encouragement. Furthermore, we need to fight against the enemy's accusations that cause division in the marriage relationship; for example, a husband that violently beats or mistreats his wife and children.

"Therefore I positioned men behind the lower parts of the wall, at the openings; and I set the people according to their families, with their swords, their spears, and their bows. And I looked, and arose and said to the nobles, to the leaders, and to the rest of the people, 'Do not be afraid of them. Remember the Lord, great and awesome, and fight for your brethren, your sons, your daughters, your wives, and your houses.'" (Nehemiah 4:13-14)

HEALTH

Some of the enemy's most deceptive weapons are sickness and accidents. A small accident caused a great division between two families. Because they were recently converted and didn't have an understanding of the Word of God, and due to their immaturity in the area of love, they cursed at each other and gave entrance to the enemy. *We then who are strong ought to bear with the scruples of the weak and not to please ourselves"* (Romans 15:1 italics added).

Many can recite 1 Corinthians 13, but in reality, how many can put it into practice? Remember, "Love suffers long and is kind; love does not envy; love does not parade itself, is not puffed up; does not behave rudely, does not seek its own, is not provoked, thinks no evil; does not rejoice in iniquity, but rejoices in the truth; bears all things, believes all things, hopes all things, endures all things" (1 Corinthians 13:4-7).

The priest of the home should pray with and over his family. Through prayer, he can bind the strongman when he brings sickness and symptoms of illness to the family members (home). Children should pray for their parents, and parents should pray for their children.

VISION

It is absolutely necessary for the Church body to submit to their leaders as long as the leadership is not contradicting or opposing the Word of God. "Can two walk together, unless they are agreed" (Amos 3:3)?

God gives a person the vision. That person then imparts and guides the people in the fulfillment of the vision. Some examples include David and Israel, Moses and the Israelites, etc. God gave me a great vision for the congregation that I pastored:

1. To reach first and second generation Hispanics through adoration, praise, preaching, and teaching of the good news.

2. To be a resource center for other churches and individuals in our community and in Latin America.

If Satan could darken, cloud, or block out our vision then, as Proverbs says, "the people will go wild," run back and forth without control. As a runaway horse cannot stop, a people without control will go wild. God builds when the people have a desire to work.

---◆---

JEALOUSY, ENVY, AND THE SPIRIT
OF ACCUSATION ARE THE GREATEST
WEAPONS FOR DIVISION

---◆---

"Also the hand of God was on Judah to give them singleness of heart to obey the command of the king and the leaders, at the word of the Lord. Now many people, a very great assembly, gathered at Jerusalem to keep the Feast of Unleavened Bread in the second month." (2 Chronicles 30:12-13)

"Behold, how good and how pleasant it is for brethren to dwell together in unity! It is like the precious oil upon the head, running down on the beard, the beard of Aaron, running down on the edge of his garments. It is like the dew of Hermon, descending upon the mountains of Zion; for there the Lord commanded the blessing – Life forevermore" (Psalm 133).

The battle is not ours; it is the Lord's! In the midst of a multitude of problems and attacks in these areas, we have God's promise that the battle is not ours, but His!

"And he said, 'Listen, all you of Judah and you inhabitants of Jerusalem, and you, king Jehoshaphat!' Thus says the Lord to you: 'Do not be afraid nor dismayed because of this great multitude, for the battle is not yours, but God's. Tomorrow go down against them. ... You will not need to fight in this battle. Position yourselves, stand still and see the salvation of the Lord, who is with you, O Judah and Jerusalem! Do not fear or be dismayed; tomorrow go out against them, for the Lord is with you.'" (2 Chronicles 20:15-17)

"You will keep him in perfect peace, whose mind is stayed on You, because he trusts in You. Trust in the Lord forever, for in You, the Lord, is everlasting strength...." (Isaiah 26:3-4)

CHAPTER TWENTY THREE

DISCOVERING PRAYER STRATEGIES

G od moves by moving people to pray. If you do not cover your pastor or your church leaders in prayer, they will not have a spiritual covering of intercession and prayer over their lives, family, and ministry.

> "Moreover He said, 'I am the God of your fathers – the God of Abraham, the God of Isaac, and the God of Jacob.' And Moses hid his face, for he was afraid to look upon God. And the Lord said: 'I have surely seen the oppression of My people who are in Egypt, and have heard their cry because of their taskmasters, for I know their sorrows. So I have come down to deliver them out of the hand of the Egyptians, and to bring them up from that land to a good and large land, to a land flowing with milk and honey, to the place of the Canaanites and the Hittites and the Amorites and the Perizzites and the Hivites and the Jebusites. Now

therefore, behold, the cry of the children of Israel has come to Me, and I have also seen the oppression with which the Egyptians oppress them. Come now, therefore, and I will send you to Pharaoh that you may bring My people, the children of Israel, out of Egypt.' But Moses said to God, 'Who am I that I should go to Pharaoh, and that I should bring the children of Israel out of Egypt?' So He said, 'I will certainly be with you. And this shall be a sign to you that I have sent you: when you have brought the people out of Egypt, you shall serve God on this mountain.'"   (Exodus 3:6-12)

Prayer is not bringing a list of needs and wants to our heavenly Father, but rather it's a revelation of God's heart for the world through the longsuffering of our own hearts.
- ◆ God's people cry out to Him.
- ◆ He hears their cries.
- ◆ He moves, guides, and saves His people from the bondage of oppression.

"And seek the peace of the city where I have caused you to be carried away captive, and pray to the Lord for it; for in its peace you will have peace." (Jeremiah 29:7)

DELIVERANCE WILL COME FROM ZION.

"Then saviors shall come to Mount Zion to judge the mountains of Esau, and the kingdom shall be the Lord's" (Obadiah 21). When God's people cry out to Him, the Spirit of the Lord is revealed and He sends a deliverer to His people.

"When the children of Israel cried out to the Lord, the Lord raised up a deliverer for the children of Israel, who delivered them: Othniel the son of Kenaz, Caleb's younger brother." (Judges 3:9)

"But when the children of Israel cried out to the Lord, the Lord raised up a deliverer for them: Ehud the son of Gera, the Benjamite, a left-handed man. By him the children of Israel sent tribute to Eglon king of Moab." (Judges 3:15)

God answers prayers by sending an anointing that destroys the strongholds and gives revelation and discernment to battle the enemy. God's people usually feel unworthy, but it's the anointing that comes in their midst that empowers them for battle. The people cried to the Lord and He sent them prophets to provide direction.

"So Israel was greatly impoverished because of the Midianites, and the children of Israel cried out to the Lord. And it came to pass, when the children of Israel cried out to the Lord because of the Midianites, that the Lord sent a prophet to the children of Israel, who said to them, 'Thus says the Lord God of Israel: I brought you up from Egypt and brought you out of the house of bondage.'" (Judges 6:6-8)

GOD'S ANOINTING FOR INTERCESSION

Cry out to the Lord and teach God's people to cry out to Him. Feel the pain and need of the city. Remember that we have a high priest that relates to us and who is sensitive to our cries. There's a prophetic anointing that comes through intercession. God's prophets will never compromise God's anointing with sin; they would rather give up their lives than give in to sin. God's people are not called to live in fear, but in confidence that God is with them. Our strength is in the calling that God has given us. Coupled with God's calling is His anointing.

GOD ANSWERS PRAYERS BY SENDING AN ANOINTING THAT DESTROYS THE STRONG-HOLDS AND GIVES REVELATION AND DISCERNMENT TO BATTLE THE ENEMY.

"Now the Angel of the Lord came and sat under the terebinth tree which was in Ophrah, which belonged to Joash the Abiezrite, while his son Gideon threshed wheat in the winepress, in order to hide it from the Midianites. And the Angel of the Lord appeared to him, and said to him, 'The Lord is with you, you mighty man of valor!' Gideon said to Him, 'O my lord, if the Lord is with us, why then has all this hapened to us? And where are all His miracles which our fathers told us about, saying, 'Did not the Lord bring us up from Egypt?' But now the Lord has forsaken us and delivered us into the hands of the Midianites.' Then the Lord turned to him and said, 'Go in this might of yours, and you shall save Israel from the hand of the Midianites. Have I not sent you?' So he said to Him, 'O my Lord, how can I save Israel? Indeed my clan is the weakest in Manasseh, and I am the least in my father's house.' And the Lord said to him, 'Surely I will be with you, and you shall defeat the Midianites as one man.'" (Judges 6:11-16)

Before we engage in spiritual warfare, we must understand that God is a God of peace and that He has called us to be peacemakers for our communities, cities, and nations. "And the God of peace will crush Satan under your feet shortly. The grace of our Lord Jesus Christ be with you. Amen." (Romans 16:20) The following three things must be in order before we engage in warfare:

1. Our focus needs to change.

The Lord first sent Gideon to his own house. While we are engaged in spiritual warfare, it's important that we also teach our children about spiritual warfare and the battle that has been waged against the family.

2. There must be unity in our intercession.

Every church member must be aware of spiritual warfare. Husbands and wives are to be the main partners in the battle within the framework of the family. As they come into unity in prayer, they are building an altar of sacrifice unto Him..

3. Our home must be in order.

God answers our prayers by lifting us up. Although oppression may strike back after we've repented, we must never give up the battle. If our homes are not in order and there is sin in the house, we hinder the Lord from working His perfect will.

"Husbands, likewise, dwell with them with understanding, giving honor to the wife, as to the weaker vessel, and as being heirs together of the grace of life, that your prayers may not be hindered." (1 Peter 3:7)

CHAPTER TWENTY FOUR

THE NEW MILLENIUM CHURCH

For I consider that the sufferings of this present time are not worthy to be compared with the glory which shall be revealed in us. For the earnest expectation of the creation eagerly waits for the revealing of the sons of God (Romans 8:18-19).

The manifestation of God's glory is beginning to take place. We are in the dawning of a new day. As the new millenium rapidly approaches us, I feel a sense of urgency that the hour has come for Jesus to be glorified through the Church, which is His body.

GOD'S CALL FOR AN AWAKENED CHURCH

God commissioned Joshua after the death of Moses to cross over the Jordan to a place where they had never been before. In the same way, God is calling His Church to recognize and listen to Him, for the hour of visitation is here.

It is the dawning of a new day, and that is why God is calling the church to awake – to get up and to engage in battle. "Proclaim ye this among the gentiles; prepare war, wake up the mighty men, let all the men of war draw near; let them come up" (Joel 3:9 King James Version).

The message of restoration is to bring unity, the power of God, and holiness into the body of Christ and to possess the nations through spiritual warfare. The word restoration in the Greek is "*katartizo*," meaning to prepare, to renew, to revive, to heal, and to perfect. God is restoring His church to its fullness, including the Prophetic and the Apostolic anointing of the early church; Ephesians 4:12 – Perfecting or Equipping; 1 Corinthians 1:10 – To be made complete (same mind, same judgement); 1 Peter 5:10 – To Perfect.

It doesn't matter what name you call it, whether it is revival, preparation, unity, or restoration; God's work is the same, and God has called us to be the forerunners of His restoration.

FIVE THINGS THE CHURCH OF THE NEW MILLENIUM WILL EXPERIENCE

1. There will be an incredible multiplication and growth in the body of Christ. This includes a dynamic growth through world evangelism and a worldwide revival. In anticipation of this, we must begin to train workers to feed and care for the multitudes of spiritual babes that will be born again into the body of Christ.

> "Before she was in labor, she gave birth; before her pain came, she delivered a male child. Who has heard such a thing? Who has seen such things? Shall the earth be made to give birth in one day? Or shall a nation be born at once? For as soon as Zion was in labor, She gave birth to her children." (Isaiah 66: 7-8)

In Psalm 2:7, the scripture speaking about a messianic declaration says: "I will declare the decree the Lord has said to Me." By declaring the decree, it became established unto Jesus as declared by the psalmist. Job 22: 28 says "You will also decree a thing, and it will be established for you." The Father essentially said to Jesus, "All you have to do is to ask me for the redemption of all mankind and I'll do it." The very last line is a direct quotation from Psalm 2:8, "Ask of me and I will give you…The very ends of the earth for your possession."

THE FATHER MUST HAVE AN INSTRUMENT THROUGH WHICH HE CAN FULFILL HIS PROMISE TO JESUS. THE ANOINTED BODY OF CHRIST IS THAT INSTRUMENT

The promise of the father was twofold. To Jesus, He promised the heathen, *the nations,* as His inheritance and the uttermost parts of the earth as His possession. To the believer, He promised the gift of the Holy Spirit. " …He commanded them not to depart from Jerusalem, but to wait for the promise of the Father, which, He said, you have heard from Me" (Acts 1.4).

The father must have an instrument through which he can fulfill his promise to Jesus. The anointed body of Christ is that instrument. The promise to the Son is to be ultimately fulfilled in the end times. Mathew 24:4 states, "And this gospel of the Kingdom shall be preached to the whole world for a witness unto all nations and then shall the end come." "You have delivered me from the strivings of the people; You have made me the head of the nations; a people I have not known shall serve me. As soon as they hear of me they obey me; the foreigners submit to me" (Psalm 18:43-44).

The contentions or strivings refer to the angry mobs crying out "Crucify Him, Crucify Him!" "A people whom I have not known shall serve me" refers to the gentiles whom God did not know under the old covenant coming into a relationship with God through Jesus Christ. Notice how quickly the heathen respond to the savior: "As soon as they hear of me, they shall obey (come under my rule) me."

2. God will send forth ministers all over the world. Especially those of the Apostolic and Prophetic, who will be instrumental in the equipping and preparation of God's army. These ministers will train God's people for the battles that are soon coming upon the earth. Ephesians states that the foundation of the church is established by the apostolic and prophetic. In the midst of the prophetic warning concerning the end-times, we have Gods promise in Daniel 11:32: "…But the people who know their God shall be strong, and carry out great exploits."

This parallels with Acts 1:8 when it refers to the power (be strong) to be my witnesses (do exploits), or 'visually manifest or do exploits that shall be a witness.'These are people who know the greatness and power of their God.

3. Great spiritual battles will take place. Intercessory prayer must increase as God's people will begin to see the power of God revealed though the prayer of faith, prophetic intercession, and apostolic intercession. "Or how can one enter a strong man's house and plunder his goods, unless he first binds the strong man? And then he will plunder his house." (Matthew 12:29)

Jesus taught that we must first **bind** the strong man before we can spoil his house. These terms refer to the old phrase 'prayer warriors.' Satan must be bound before captives can be set free from his hold; the strong man must be bound. "Assuredly, I say to you, whatever you bind on earth will be bound in heaven, and whatever you loose on earth will be loosed in heaven" (Matthew 18:18).

4. There will be a new unity in the body. It has always had the unity of the faith, but now it will come into the unity of spirit. The church will enjoy its glorious hour until we all attain the fullness of the measure of Christ.

5. The glory of the Lord will be manifested. The glory of the Lord, which is a reflection of God's character, will be manifested as the church begins to move in love, compassion, consecration, and dedication. God's power anointing and excellence will be restored to God's people, not because God has removed it, but because God's people will consecrate and separate themselves unto the things of God. "And the glory which You gave Me I have given them, that they may be one just as You and I are one" (John 17:22).

"Arise, shine; for thy light has come! And the glory of the lord is risen upon you. For, behold, the darkness shall cover the earth, and gross darkness the people: But the Lord shall arise over you. And His glory will be seen upon you. The Gentiles shall come to your light, and kings to the brightness of your rising. Lift up your eyes all around, and see: They all gather together, they come to you; your sons shall come from afar, and thy daughters shall be nursed by your side." (Isaiah 60:1-4)

"For thus says the Lord of hosts: 'Once more (it is a little while) I will shake the heavens and earth, and dry land; and I will shake all nations, and they shall come to the Desire of All nations, and I will fill this temple with glory,' says the Lord of hosts. 'The silver is Mine and the gold is Mine,' says the Lord of hosts. 'The glory of the latter temple shall be greater than of the former,' says the Lord of hosts; ' And in this place I will give peace,' says the Lord of hosts." (Haggai 2:6-9)

Bob Weiner, Founder of Maranatha Ministries, said there are three keys to the restoration of God's people:
♦ **Christians must have a sense of dominion.** He has given us the authority to rule over the earth. "The earth is the Lord's, and all its fullness, The world and those who dwell therein." (Psalm 24.1)
♦ **Christians must operate with God's love and compassion.** We must be imitators of Christ so that faith will operate through love. It was through His love and compassion that Jesus brought about his miracles. "But when He saw the multitudes, He was moved with compassion for them, because they were weary and scattered, like sheep having no shepherd." (Matthew 9:36)
♦ **The body of Christ must have a message**. It must testify through its words, actions, and deeds what it means to be a Christian. We are called to have impact. We must be a voice crying in the wilderness. We must be the conscience of our nation. We must not be passive on issues such as abortion, genocide, homosexuality, pornography, secular humanism, the occult, sexual liberation, religious cults, violence, corruption, idolatry, and anything that is condemned by the word of God.

It was because of the apathy of the people that Israel fell into apostasy and compromised God's calling. We must blow the trumpet unto the nations. We must speak out for the repentance of our nation and restoration of the biblical principles under which it was founded.

"Is this not the fast that I have chosen: To loose the bonds of wickedness, To undo the heavy burdens, To let the oppressed go free, And that you break every yoke? Is it not to share your bread with the hungry, And that you bring to your house the poor who are cast out; When you see the naked, that you cover him, And not hide yourself from your own flesh? Then your light shall break forth like the morning, Your healing shall spring forth speedily, And your righteousness shall go before you; The glory of the Lord shall be your rear guard. Then you shall call, and the Lord will answer; You shall cry, and He will say, 'Here I am.' "If you take away the yoke from your midst, The pointing of the finger, and speaking wickedness. If you extend your soul to the hungry And satisfy the afflicted soul, Then your light shall dawn in the darkness, And your darkness shall be as the noonday. The Lord will guide you continually, And satisfy your soul in drought, And strengthen your bones; You shall be like a watered garden, And like a spring of water, whose waters do not fail. Those from among you Shall build the old waste places; You shall raise up the foundations of many generations; And you shall be called the Repairer of the Breach, The Restorer of the Streets to Dwell In." (Isaiah 58:6-12)

APPENDIX ONE

THE STUDY GUIDE

INTRODUCTION

1. What is the Spirit saying to the church today?

2. What perceptions have we had of the church in the past?

3. According to George Otis, Jr., what are the three crucial elements for the church today?

4. What are the three institutions (organizations) that Satan wants to destroy to hinder the fulfillment of the Great Commission?

5. Why are you interested in spiritual warfare?

THE THREE LEVELS OF SPIRITUAL WARFARE CHAPTER 1

1. Define the 'strongholds' that Satan uses in spiritual warfare.

2. Define the three types of 'spirits' the Bible mentions.

3. What stronghold are we fighting against in the con-

flict against Satan on the earthly level? What institution (organization) is aimed in this area of combat?

4. What strongholds are we fighting in the conflict against Satan on the spiritual level? What institution (organization) is aimed in this area of combat?

5. What strongholds are we fighting against in the conflict against Satan on the strategic level?

6. What institution (organization) is aimed in this area of combat?

7. What did Jesus come for?

8. What is the purpose of Spiritual Warfare?

OFFENSIVE WARFARE
CHAPTER 2

1. What is God's call to the Church?

2. First of all, what is needed to fulfill this call?

3. What are the things that every person seeks after?

4. What are the four 'must haves' that God looks for in every Christian?

5. What are the seven things God requires of His Church and the members of His body?

6. What type of ministers is God looking for?

JESUS AND THE CHURCH ON THE OFFENSIVE
CHAPTER 3

1. On what level did Jesus' public ministry begin?

2. Why was Jesus revealed? Give two Biblical references that demonstrate the purpose of His coming.

3. According to W. E. Vines' *Expository Dictionary of the New Testament*, what does the term '**desert**' mean?

4. Give three biblical references that reveal that Jesus delegated authority to believers over the powers of the enemy.

5. How does the Bible refer to Satan, even after the cross? Give Biblical references.

6. What is Satan's main objective?

7. Read Jeremiah 1:10; define these terms:

    a. Pluck up:

    b. Break down:

    c. Destroy:

    d. Overthrow:

    e. Edify:

    f. Plant:

SATAN'S TACTICS
CHAPTERS 4-5

1. Define the term '**schemes**':

2. According to the Bible, what was the first institution that God blessed? Give a scriptural reference.

3. What concepts do we learn regarding the development of our family?

4. According to 1 John 2:16, how does Satan destroy human relations with the family and with God?

5. How does the attack against the believer come?

6. According to Ephesians 6:12, as Christians our warfare is against who?

7. According to 2 Corinthians 10:3-5, what types of weapons have been given to us and what is our battle?

8. What weapons has God given us for spiritual warfare?

9. According to *Nehemiah 4:14*, what does God call us to? For whom?

10. What is Satan's main tactic and what are the results of that tactic?

SPIRITUAL WARFARE IN THE BATTLEFIELD
CHAPTER 6

1. Read 1 Corinthians 2:11-14. What are the three spirits mentioned in this scripture?

2. What laws do each of these spirits obey?

3. According to 1 Thessalonians 5:23, the totality of a human being consists in what?

4. What is man's conscience called in the New Testament? Give three Bible references.

5. Define the following Greek terms:
   a. *Pneuma*
   b. *Psyche*
   c. *Soma*

6. According to Galatians 5, what are the works of the **flesh** and their fruit?

7. According to Galatians 5, what are the works of the **Spirit** and their fruit?

Spirits Unleashed Against the Church
Chapters 7-11

1. Which spirits are unleashed to destroy the family?

2. What are the consequences of deceit and hardening of the heart?

3. Define the terms 'spirit of accusation' and 'spirit of rejection.'

4. Which spirits are unleashed to destroy the church?

5. Define the term **'spirit'** according to W.E. Vine's *Dictionary of the New Testament.*

6. What are the characteristics of the spirit of Antichrist?

7. What are the characteristics of the spirit of Absalom?

8. What are the characteristics of the spirit of Lethargy?

9. What are the consequences of the stronghold of a love gone cold?

10. What are the consequences of the spirit of accusation?

11. What are the characteristics of the spirit of Jezebel?

12. List 10 spirits unleashed against the Church.

13. List 10 spirits given to the Christian to counterattack the enemy's attacks.

SPIRITUAL MAPPING
CHAPTERS 12-13

1. Define spiritual mapping.

2. Why is spiritual mapping important?

3. Define the term **'territorial spirits.'**

4. Why is it important to identify and know the past?

5. How do satanic powers enthrone themselves over different geographic zones?

6. What influence has the spirit of destruction had in Latin America?

7. What are the initial three steps to enter into spiritual warfare?

THE WEAPONS OF OUR WARFARE
CHAPTER 14

1. What are the weapons of warfare that God has given us for the battle?

2. Define the Greek term *'energeo.'*

3. Define the Greek term *'kratos.'*

4. Define the Greek term *'Ischus.'*

5. According to Paul's letter to the Ephesians, of what does the armor of God consist?

PRAYER STRATEGIES
CHAPTERS 15-16

1. What are the results of intercession in evangelism and missions?

2. What does the term **'bind the strongman'** mean?

3. Define intercession and intercessor.

4. What does the term **'strategy'** mean?

5. List three foundational truths for a victorious battle.

6. According to the Bible, list 5 elements of our call to prayer.

PULLING DOWN STRONGHOLDS WITH INTERCESSION
CHAPTER 17

1. For what purpose is God raising an army?

2. As soldiers in God's army, what steps should we take to pray for our cities and nations?

3. What is the difference between prayer and intercession?

4. Why is it that most of the time we cannot destroy strongholds?

5. List the 4 elements of the plan of resistance.

PULLING DOWN STRONGHOLDS WITH FASTING
CHAPTER 18

1. What is the meaning of '**fasting**?'

2. List 5 results of fasting.

3. How should we fast?

4. List 4 different ways to fast.

5. According to *Isaiah 58*, what is the fast that Jehovah wants?

PULLING DOWN STRONGHOLDS WITH PRAISE AND WORSHIP
CHAPTER 19

1. Why do we praise and worship God?

2. What is the true meaning of worship?

3. What are the results of praise to God?

4. What power is there in praise?

5. List the 5 Hebrew words that translate into praise and their meanings.

6. List 8 different forms of praising and worshipping.

PULLING DOWN STRONGHOLDS WITH THE NAME OF JESUS CHAPTER 20

1. In which ways can a name be inherited?

2. What authority is there in the name of Jesus?

3. What are the meanings of Jesus, Jehovah, and Joshua?

4. What happens when a Christian uses the name of Jesus?

5. Write a brief personal testimony about the use of the name of Jesus in your prayer life.

VULNERABLE AREAS IN SPIRITUAL BATTLE CHAPTER 22

1. How does the apostle Peter describe the adversary?

2. List 5 areas in which the enemy works to injure the Christian.

3. What happens when there is not a godly vision?

4. Briefly write regarding the events in 2 Chronicles 2:20.

Discovering Prayer Strategies
Chapter 23

1. What is Prayer?

2. How does God answer prayer?

3. List three things we must do before we enter into prayer.

The New Millenium Church
Chapter 24

1. What is the purpose of the message of *Restoration?*

2. List five things the Church of the New Millenium will experience.

3. What are the three keys to the *restoration* of God's people?

RIDDING YOUR HOME OF SPIRITUAL DARKNESS

Chuck D. Pierce
& Rebecca Wagner Sytsema

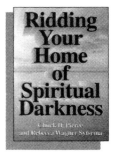

Christians are often completely unaware of how the enemy has gained access to their homes through what they own. This practical, easy-to-read book can be used by any Christian to pray through their home and property in order to close the door to the enemy and experience richer spiritual life. Included are chapters on children, sin, generational curses, and spiritual discernment, as well as a step-by-step guide to praying through your home and a section of questions and answers.
Paperback (75 pp.) • 0.9667481.7.4 • **$7.20 (save 10%)**

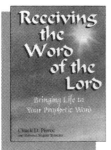

RECEIVING THE WORD OF THE LORD

Chuck D. Pierce
& Rebecca Wagner Sytsema

The Bible makes it very clear that God has a plan for our lives. By hearing and receiving the voice of God, we can know our purpose and destiny. In this book you will discover how to hear the voice of God, develop an understanding of prophecy, learn how to test a prophetic word, and experience the joy of responding to God's voice.
Paperback (41 pp.) • 0.9667481.2.3 • **$5.40 (save 10%)**

From C. Peter Wagner . . .

RADICAL HOLINESS
FOR RADICAL LIVING
C. Peter Wagner

Can anyone really live a holy life? Is there a test of holiness? *Radical Holiness for Radical Living* answers these and other questions as it opens the way for you to move to new levels in your Christian life. You can defeat Satan's schemes and enjoy daily victory in your walk with God.
Paperback (41 pp.) · 0.9667481.1.5 · **$5.40 (save 10%)**

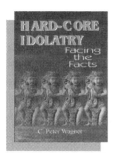

HARD-CORE IDOLATRY:
FACING THE FACTS
C. Peter Wagner

This hard-hitting book is destined to clear away the foggy thinking about idolatry that has permeated churches today. This book will help you recognize idolatry (even in some of our churches), confront the schemes of the enemy with more understanding and power, feel the pain of God's broken heart when His people worship idols, and begin to cleanse your home of idolatrous objects.
Paperback (43 pp.) · 0.9667481.4.X · **$5.40 (save 10%)**

REVIVAL! IT CAN
TRANSFORM YOUR CITY
C. Peter Wagner

This book answers many questions including: What exactly is revival? Can my city actually be transformed through revival? What steps can be taken to sustain revival in a city? Discover how the Spirit of God can visibly transform our cities through the revival for which we have been praying!
Paperback (63 pp.) · 0.9667481.8.2 · **$5.40 (save 10%)**

HOW TO CAST OUT DEMONS: A BEGINNER'S GUIDE

Doris M. Wagner

Many modern Christians are now agreeing that we should take Jesus' command to cast out demons more seriously than we have. But how do we do it? Where do we start? This practical, down-to-earth book, written by a respected deliverance practitioner, will show you how.

This one-of-a-kind book will help you to:

♦ Take authority over demonic spirits
♦ Conduct a private 2-hour prayer appointment
♦ Administer a 15-page diagnostic questionnaire
♦ Break bondages of rejection, addiction, lust, and more
♦ Bring inner healing and break soul ties
♦ Set free those whom the enemy has held captive

All this rooted in solid, biblical integrity and done in a calm, safe, controlled ministry environment.

Paperback (201 pp.) • 1.58502.002.8 • **$10.80 (save 10%)**

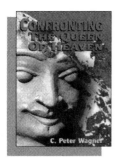

CONFRONTING THE QUEEN OF HEAVEN

C. Peter Wagner

This book takes a look at what is perhaps one of the most powerful spirits in Satan's hierarchy--the Queen of Heaven. This book answers what we as Christians can do to play a part in confronting the Queen of Heaven and proclaiming that Jesus Christ is Lord.

Paperback (42 pp.) • 0.9667481.3.1 • **$5.40 (save 10%)**

PRAYING THROUGH TURKEY
AN INTERCESSOR'S GUIDE TO AN ANCIENT AND NEEDY LAND
Andrew Jackson with George Otis, Jr.

This book will take you on a fantastic journey, tracing Christianity from its roots to modern times in the nation of Turkey. Intercessors will receive invaluable instruction on how to pray for the cities and unreached peoples of Turkey.

Paperback (60 pp.) • 1.58502.000.1 • **$5.40 (save 10%)**

Coming soon from Wagner Institute Publishing:

♦ SUPERNATURAL ARCHITECTURE
  by Dr. Stan DeKoven

♦ HOW TO HAVE A DYNAMIC CHURCH PRAYER MINISTRY, *by Jill Griffith*

♦ THE STRATEGIC PRAYER ROOM
  by Chuck D. Pierce & Rebecca Wagner Sytsema

For credit card orders please:
call *toll free* 1-888-563-5150
or fax 1-719-266-8256
or email: Arsenal@cpwagner.net

Or mail order with payment to:
The Arsenal
P.O. Box 62958
Colorado Springs, CO 80962-2958 USA

For bulk orders please:
call: 1-719-277-6776
or email: WIsales@cpwagner.net

All international orders must be paid by credit card

Name _____

Street Address _____
(Cannot deliver to P.O. Box)

_____

Phone _____

Title	Product Number	Qty.	Total
	Subtotal (carry this amount to other side)		

Order form continued . . .

Shipping Rate Table for US only		Subtotal (from other side)	
Amt. of Subtotal	Add		
$50 and under	$5		
$50.01-$60.00	$6	CO residents add 6.01% sales tax	
$60.01-$80.00	$8		
$80.01-$100.00	$10		
Over $100.00	10% of order		
For international orders, please call or fax with credit card. Shipping will be calculated for you.		Shipping (see table)	
		Donation to GHM	
		TOTAL ENCLOSED (US FUNDS ONLY)	

Please allow 10 days for delivery. International orders may require
6 weeks for delivery.

METHOD OF PAYMENT:
☐ Check/Money Order (made payable to The Arsenal)
☐ Credit Card: ☐ ☐ ☐

Number:_____

Exp. Date:_____ Signature: _____